CHOICE

STUDIES IN
PHILOSOPHICAL PSYCHOLOGY

Edited by

R. F. HOLLAND

CHOICE
The Essential Element in Human Action

by
ALAN DONAGAN

ROUTLEDGE & KEGAN PAUL
LONDON AND NEW YORK

First published in 1987 by
Routledge & Kegan Paul Ltd
11 New Fetter Lane, London EC4P 4EE

Published in the USA by
Routledge & Kegan Paul Inc.
in association with Methuen Inc.,
29 West 35th Street, New York, NY 10001

Set in 10/12 Baskerville
by Falcon Graphic Art Ltd
and printed in Great Britain
by T J Press (Padstow) Ltd
Padstow, Cornwall

Library of Cataloguing in Publication Data
Donagan, Alan.
Choice, the essential element in human action.
(Studies in philosophical psychology)
Bibliography: p.
Includes index.
1. Act (Philosophy) 2. Choice (Psychology)
3. Will. I. Title II. Series.
B105.A35D66   1987   128'3   86-33895
British Library CIP Data also available
ISBN 0-7102-1168-6

For
GILBERT RYLE
Of Happy Memory

CONTENTS

PREFACE

This book was planned twenty years ago, when I was working on what became *The Theory of Morality* (Chicago: University of Chicago Press, 1977). Since *ought* implies *can*, writings about morality presuppose much about human action. Yet although conclusions about action can defensibly be drawn from established moral theory, no moral theory can become established unless its presuppositions about action can be defended independently.

Human beings, so far as their history is known, have always distinguished human doings that are actions from those that are not, and have interpreted those that are actions by ascribing to their doers a complex mental life. The beliefs in terms of which members of one society do so are intelligible to members of others, and the bulk are common to members of all. Since the philosophy of human action is an analytical exploration of these bodies of beliefs, it should not surprise us that its foundations were laid by Plato and Aristotle, and have endured.

The philosophy of action has developed, less because the material available for study has grown (although of course it has), than because advances in philosophy generally (themselves affected by advances in the sciences) have equipped us to probe it more deeply.

Earlier books in this series have mostly aspired to make use

of what has been called 'the legacy of Wittgenstein'. I hope
that this one will not be read as repudiating that legacy. In
studying Wittgenstein's writings, I seldom dissent from what I
read. However, I have been disappointed to find that many of
my answers to the questions he constantly puts to his readers
are not those of others. I refer to his writings rarely, not
because they have not influenced me, but in order not to be
drawn into quarrelling about what they mean.

My debt, personal as well as philosophical, to Gilbert Ryle,
my supervisor at Oxford, cannot be reckoned. How much I
owe him philosophically may be concealed from those for
whom *The Concept of Mind* is at bottom behaviourist: to me it is
a classic of modern analytic Aristotelianism, dressed in a
behaviourism now out of style.

My other chief debts are to two of the greatest of contemporary philosophers, Roderick Chisholm and Donald Davidson,
whose seminars I have been able, at different times, to attend
as a colleague. It is a comfort that, when I venture to differ
from one of them, I can sometimes claim the support of the
other. Unfortunately for me, although I heard G.E.M.
Anscombe lecture on Wittgenstein's *Investigations* in 1953, I
have never been in a position to attend any of her classes on
the theory of action.

On the questions I try to answer, the ideas I appropriate
from others are acknowledged by my references. Since I quote
from Donald Davidson, Anthony Kenny and John Searle more
extensively than from anybody else, it seemed courteous to
seek their permission to do so, and I thank them for according
it. Such references, however, do not mention everybody from
whom I learned to ask the questions I do. Many of those
questions would not have been asked but for the writings, and
in some cases the conversation, of Arthur Danto, A.I. Melden,
Wilfrid Sellars and G.H. von Wright.

The John Simon Guggenheim Foundation awarded me a
Fellowship for 1976–7 to complete my work on action theory,

which, together with a Fellowship from the Center of Advanced Study in the Behavioral Sciences at Stanford, and a supplementary grant from the University of Chicago, enabled me to try to do so in ideal circumstances. The result was a fresh start.

Many of my fellow-students at the uncounted philosophical gatherings at which I have been present when human action was discussed have made a difference to what I have written. Among those many debts, two stand out. Marilyn and Robert Adams criticized in detail the penultimate version of the present study in a seminar at UCLA they attended. And corrections of what I thought would be the final text were made by members of two seminars in which it was critically discussed: one at Wheaton College arranged by Arthur Holmes; and the other at Fred Stoutland's house at Ottertail Lake, attended by members of Saint Olaf College and of Carleton College.

Pasadena   A.D.
November 1986

CHAPTER 1

RATIONAL ANIMALS AND THEIR ACTIONS

A. *The Socratic tradition in the theory of human action*

The philosophical theory of human action begins with Plato. In a passage in the *Phaedo* he presents Socrates as making fun of Anaxagoras for announcing that he would explain the structure of the universe as ordered by mind for the best, and then producing a physical theory of it.

> It seemed to me [he makes Socrates say] . . . very much as if one should say that Socrates does with intelligence whatever he does, and then, in trying to give the causes (*aitias*) of the particular thing I do, should say first that I am now sitting here because my body is composed of bones and sinews . . .; and so, as the bones are hung loose in their ligaments, the sinews, by relaxing and contracting, make me able to bend my limbs now, and that is the cause of my sitting here with my legs bent. Or as if in the same way he should give voice and air and hearing and countless other things of the sort as causes (*aitias*) for our talking with each other, and should fail to mention the real causes (*alethos aitias*), which are, that the Athenians decided it was best to condemn me, and therefore I have decided that it was best for me to sit here, and that it is right for me to stay and undergo whatever penalty they order. For, by the dog, I fancy these bones and sinews of mine would have been in Megara or Boeotia long ago, carried thither by an opinion (*doxes*) of what is best, if I did not think it was better and nobler to endure any

penalty the city may inflict rather than to escape and run away. But it is most absurd to call things of that sort causes (*aitia*). If anyone were to say that I could not have done what I thought proper if I had not bones and sinews and other things that I have, he would be right. But to say that those things are the cause of my doing what I do, and that I act with intelligence but not from the choice of what is best (*tou beltistou hairesei*), would be an extremely careless way of talking (98c–99a).

Two things Socrates says in this passage are pregnant. The first, which is partly implicit, is that tracing the physical chain of causation from his sitting in prison to relaxings and contractings of his sinews, and those to some other happenings in his body (as modern neurophysiology would to certain neuronal discharges in his cerebral cortex), while useful as far as it goes, does not explain the first link in the chain. And although many neurophysiologists believe that one day complete neurophysiological explanations of human behaviour will be possible, others do not. Socrates would have been an unbeliever. His second pregnant observation was that the cause of his sitting in prison was perfectly well known to all his friends: namely that he had decided that it was better to submit to the punishment to which he had been lawfully if unjustly sentenced than to escape. This explanation, although not physical, is both true and sufficient.

Yet Socrates did not reinstate, even for human actions, the doctrine he ridiculed Anaxagoras for abandoning: that things are to be explained by showing that they are for the best. The cause of his remaining in prison is that he decided that it was best to do so; but deciding that something is so is not the same as its being so, even if you are Socrates. In the *Crito*, Plato presents Socrates as arguing that his reasons for remaining in prison are good reasons; but his explanation would hold even if they had been bad. His friends, before the discussion reported in the *Crito*, believed it to be for the best that he escape; and in his position they presumably would have escaped. The falsity of their pre-*Crito* belief about what would be for the best would not have impaired its power to affect their conduct. At most, Socrates establishes that human actions are explained by showing, not that they are for the best, but that those who do them believe that they are for the best.

Does his conclusion hold only for human beings? Only human beings remain in prison because they believe that it is better to obey the law than to run away; yet many higher animals, rabbits for example, will risk death in order to defend their young, rather than escape to safety. Are we to say that their doings are likewise to be explained by what they believe to be for the best? Plato offered no theory of animal behaviour; but his successor Aristotle did. His development of Socrates' teaching about the explanation of human action was part of a comprehensive biology; and the structure of that biology, as a classification of the various forms of living things, still largely stands.

According to Aristotle, all beings that are individuals, as distinct from mere parcels of stuff (drops of water, heaps of sand, and the like), are living; and the most primitive living things are plants. A plant is an organized physical object – a body – that normally develops through certain definite stages, namely, those characteristic of its species; and its life is primarily its power to develop through those stages by taking in suitable matter from its surroundings (air, food and drink) and transforming it into the kinds of material of which its body is composed at each stage.

Plants have life-histories. They sink roots, grow, sprout leaves and shed them, bring forth seeds and scatter them, and in the end die. Like plants, animals transform food, grow, reproduce and die; but they are marked off from plants by their powers of sense (even the most primitive animal has the sense of touch); and their life-histories differ from those of plants in consisting in part of responses to what they sense. Moreover, while the responses of the lower animals to what they sense, of shellfish and worms for example, are rigidly fixed, some of those of higher animals show them to be aware of others as possible. As Stephen Clark points out, 'the macaque who found out how to separate wheat from sand by throwing handfuls of the two combined into the sea' discerned a possibility different from that of trying to pick the wheat from the sand grain by grain (Clark, 22); and every dog lover has his tales to tell.

Aristotle nevertheless maintains that the complex activities by which the higher animals surprise and intrigue even those who do not love them can all be explained on the hypothesis that they can form images of what they have sensed, and desire to do or not to do some of the things they imagine themselves as doing. Their powers of imagining what they can do vary in effectiveness. A cat, seeing a mouse, may imagine itself both as pouncing on it and as simply watching it. If it desires to pounce more than to watch, it will pounce. Yet if its power to imagine what it can do is defective, it will not land on the mouse as it imagines itself doing; and its subsequent behaviour will betray its frustration. An imaginative capacity that elicits desire in this way was called by the medieval Aristotelians an 'estimative power' (Aquinas (1), I, 78, 4; cf. (2), III, lect. 6). That power is found in human animals as well as in nonhuman ones, most notably in great craftsmen, in artists working in physical media, and in athletes; but that some of their activities are exercises of that power is not what is characteristically human about them.

Part of human behaviour, according to Aristotle, cannot be explained in this way. Unlike all or most animal behaviour, it is elicited by intellectual representations, not by sensory or imaginative ones. Intellect is the power to represent possibilities, not in sensory images but in propositions that are true or false. Once a proposition has been thought of, it is possible to take various attitudes towards it: that of accepting it (or its contradictory) as true; that of hoping or fearing that it (or its contradictory) is true, and so forth. Bertrand Russell happily described the attitudes thus taken as 'propositional attitudes', and his locution is now common. Propositional attitudes are characteristically referred to by using 'such words as "believe", "desire", "doubt", all of which, when they occur in a sentence, must be followed by a subordinate sentence telling what it is that is believed or desired or doubted' (Russell (2), 65; cf. 167– 9).

In treating both sensation and imagination on one hand, and intellect on the other, as powers or capacities to represent a world of which their possessors are a part, Aristotle differed not only from his great teacher Plato, but also from many later thinkers in all periods. And in treating the propounding of propositions as the sole representative exercise of the intellectual power, so that all attitudes to intellectual representations are to propositions, that is, to representations having one of two semantic values, truth or falsity, Russell and most Aristotelians differ both from those for whom thinking is not representative, and from those for whom representation is not propositional – which includes many who would style themselves rationalists, as well as empiricists in the tradition of Locke.

One of the most original and thoroughly elaborated of contemporary theories of action, that of Hector-Neri Castaneda, is anti-Aristotelian on both counts. According to it, thinking does not represent the world, but directly presents it – the world itself consisting of proposition-like entities called guises. And attitudes to presentations are not confined to those that are true or false: there are presentations that have a semantic value other than truth or falsity, namely, legitimacy or illegitimacy. Castaneda calls them 'practitions' (see Castaneda (1), *passim*; and (2), 395–409). Obviously, intermediate lines of thought are open: for example, you might reject Castaneda's anti-representationalism, but distinguish practitions from propositions as a second variety of representation.

If philosophical investigations of specific topics were required to go deeply into the current work in semantics and ontology on which they draw, there would be few of them. Yet any such investigation that uses the semantical and ontological results of others tests them indirectly: on one hand, if it succeeds in solving its problems, whatever faults the results it uses may have were not serious enough to invalidate it; and on the other, if it fails, its failure may be traceable to faults in them. As will appear throughout what follows, since much of the content of any theory of action has counterparts in other theories, it can make use of them, even though they draw upon different semantical and ontological positions. Some of my reasons for adhering to Aristotle and Russell in treating human actions as arising out of propositional attitudes will also appear. But readers should be aware that, at this point, investigation could take another direction.

While speaking of attitudes to propositions is intelligible in ordinary educated speech, it is hard to say exactly what propositions are. Bertrand Russell confidently declared that 'propositions . . . are to be defined as psychological occurrences of certain sorts – complex images, expectations, etc. Such occurrences are "expressed" by sentences, but the sentences "assert" something else. When two sentences have the same meaning, that is because they express the same proposition' (Russell (2), 189). In other words, when somebody utters a sentence he as a rule 'asserts' his belief that what his sentence 'expresses' is true; and what his sentence expresses is as a rule expressed by any other sentence having the same meaning. The belief he thus asserts is not the sentence in which he expresses it, because that same belief can be expressed in a language he does not know.

This ready and easy way of elucidating what propositions are is not final. If propositions are identified as what is expressed by sets of sentences having the same sense, and if sentences having the same sense are identified as those that correctly translate one another, it would be viciously circular to identify a correct translation of a given sentence as one that expresses the same proposition or preserves the same sense. But how otherwise is a correct translation to be identified?

All contemporary work on this question begins with W.V. Quine's classic exploration in *Word and Object*. Quine began by inquiring how a field linguist, say a sixteenth-century Portuguese Jesuit, might construct a manual for translating into a tongue familiar to him, say Latin, utterances in one that was utterly unfamiliar, say Japanese. Assuming that the utterances of the Japanese were linguistic, and that most of them, like most of ours, express propositional attitudes, he would try to learn their language by imitating suitable speakers of it and attending to their responses. And, since propositions are true or false, he would begin by trying to pick out those that express beliefs, because an utterance expressing a belief must consist wholly or in large part of an expression of the proposition believed. Simple beliefs about objects both he and his Japanese interlocutors could see and touch would be best.

If the linguist can assume that an utterance by a Japanese interlocutor who is pointing to something expresses a true belief about it, he can reflect on the beliefs he himself might express in the same situation, and test whether expressions of any of them will do as translations. His method would be simple, if laborious. He would provisionally suppose that the Japanese speaker's utterance resembles his proposed Latin translation in structure, and observing what further utterances with some of the same elements, whether by him or them, his Japanese interlocutors also seem to believe, he would propose translations of those further utterances in which any elements occurring in the earlier ones would be translated in the same way. If, by amending some proposals that do not work, and discarding others, he arrives at a scheme by which all the utterances in Japanese he has heard or made can be rendered, their number being large, and by which few or none that express something the Japanese seem to believe are translated into Latin sentences which he disbelieves, he has modest reason to be confident that his scheme is on sound lines.

Of course, he may be ludicrously wrong. That an uttered sentence and an uttered would-be translation of it are believed by speaker and translator alike are very thin evidence that the one translates the other correctly. This is most obvious when, without being aware of it, the translator disbelieves what the native speaker is saying, and desperately tries to render it into something he believes. In setting out on their enterprise, translators cannot be assured of success. However, if a linguist arrives at a position in which he himself can produce an extensive array of utterances, in a language formerly unknown to him, to which native speakers of it respond in such a way that his utterances and their responses, when rendered into one of his languages according to his translation scheme, constitute an intelligible exchange of opinion, it is unlikely that his and their beliefs and interests so diverge that his scheme is wholly astray. As Davidson has observed, 'very thin evidence in support of a each of a potential infinity of points can yield rich results, even with respect to the points' (Davidson (2), 137).

If you cling to the popular intuitive notion that the Japanese sentences thus translated must each express a proposition that is expressed by members of at most one set of more or less synonymous Latin sentences, you cannot escape concluding that the Japanese learn their mother tongue in some other way than by observing how their fellows use it and how they react to the utterances of those learning it. Frege, for example, because he speaks of the senses of sentences and their parts as belonging to a third realm, alongside the physical realm and the realm of sensation and feeling, and directly accessible to us, is commonly held to have believed that we have access to that world otherwise than by reflecting on evidence about linguistic usage.

It is more charitable, and not less intelligent, to treat the Fregean sense of a sentence as what is captured by any rendering of it into another language that accords with a translation scheme that satisfies all the available tests. That this is less determinate than Frege thought, because there are several such schemes, should not trouble us: it is determinate enough for communication. As Davidson has remarked, 'Indeterminacy of meaning or translation does not represent a failure to capture significant distinctions; it marks the fact that certain apparent distinctions are not significant' (Davidson (2), 154). Over and above what can be learned by speakers of a language in interpreting one another's utterances, there is no fact of the matter about what their utterances mean.

Quine went on to declare that the concept of a proposition, and *a fortiori* that of a propositional attitude, have no place in serious philosophy (Quine (1), 218–21). It is true that, when meaning is the 'object of philosophical and scientific clarification and analysis', as it is in *Word and Object*, it and its relatives are for that very reason 'ill-suited for use as . . . instrument[s]' of that analysis (Quine (2), 185). But it does not follow that the 'worthy object' of one philosophical analysis may not be a proper instrument in the analysis of some quite different object, say human action.

Nothing in Quine's investigation shows that the propositions to which human beings take attitudes are not determinate enough for their attitudes to them to explain their actions (Davidson (2), 239–41). Nor does anything in it show that those propositions, or the senses of their constituents, do not belong to a third realm, distinct both from that of physical happenings and from that of sensation and feeling, as long as that realm is acknowledged to be collaboratively created by human beings in communicating with one another linguistically. Propositions, as they will be understood in what follows, cannot exist without beings who communicate linguistically, and there is no access to them except by way of that communication.

B.   Should the Socratic tradition be jettisoned as folk psychology?

Philosopher-psychologists such as Myles Brand, Paul Church-land and Stephen Stich disparage research on Socratic lines into human action as stagnant. Although for two millennia, historians, philosophers, and psychologists working in motivation theory have been explaining human action on the presupposition that it largely arises from propositional attitudes, they not unreasonably contend that 'we are negligibly better at explaining human behaviour in . . . terms [of that presupposition] than was Sophocles' (Churchland, 75). Now, however, times are changing. The most enterprising psychological research is being done by psychologists who dismiss reference to propositional attitudes as rooted in prescientific folk beliefs, having no better claim to scientific respect than folk medicine. Philosophers should take example by them, and jettison propositional attitudes as useless relics of 'folk psychology'.

What weight the complaint has that we are negligibly better at explaining human action in terms of propositional attitudes than was Sophocles depends on how well Sophocles did it. Some consider that Sophocles did it well, and doubt whether scientific psychology will ever do much better.

Churchland may possibly be right in asserting that an explanatory psychology of all human behaviour can be developed. But he has given no reason at all to believe that there is anything wrong with the concepts of action developed in our culture for the conduct of practical affairs. Socrates dismissed the search for physical explanations of why he remained in prison on the twofold ground that nobody had found any that were adequate, and that numerous explanations of human actions by reference to propositional attitudes are both well established and adequate. Churchland, in objecting that explanations of the Socratic sort will not do because they fail to suggest physical explanatory hypotheses, betrays that he has utterly missed the point.

Stich has not only seen the point Churchland missed (Stich, 212–14), but has gone on to acknowledge that, unless it provides rival and better explanations of significant human actions, scientific psychology cannot effectively object to 'folk' explanations of them in terms of propositional attitudes. Does it provide them? Does it even promise to? The answer that can be collected from Stich's circumspect survey of the present state of psychology in *From Folk Psychology to Cognitive Science* is confessedly ambiguous.

After the demise of behaviourism, according to Stich, psychologists recognized both that the scientific psychology must inquire into the kinds of human activity with which behaviourism failed: namely, those familiarly described in terms of propositional attitudes. Some of them therefore decided to treat the traditional concepts of belief, desire, intention and the like as functional, and as applying to events in the human central nervous system that are causually connected with observable behaviour, and to devise testable explanatory hypotheses in terms of these principles. Cognitive psychology was the result. 'We now have', Stich tells us, 'theories of reasoning, problem-solving, inference, perception, imagery, memory and more, all cast in the common-sense idiom. . . . The use of this workaday "mentalistic" folk vocabulary has become one of the hallmarks of the burgeoning field of cognitive science' (Stich, 4–5).

If the Socratic programme were stagnant, as Stich believes, the case for a cognitive psychology in terms of propositional attitudes would be very strong. The variety of such a psychology that is best known, partly because of his brilliant and engaging presentation of it, is Jerry Fodor's (cf. Fodor). True, it has features which many of his colleagues find unpalatable, such as postulating an inner language in which all human minds conduct their operations. Nevertheless, if there is a case for a cognitive psychology at all, there are good general reasons to expect that it will turn out to be in terms of propositional attitudes, quite apart from any particular research programme (see e.g. Horgan and Woodward).

Yet although many cognitive psychologists are confident that scientific psychology will thus be reconciled with philosophical tradition, Stich believes it more probable than not that their hope will turn out to be a cheat. In much of the best work that is now being done, he contends, the traditional expressions for propositional attitudes, while used, do not bear their traditional meanings. 'As I see it,' he writes, 'the notion of "content" or the . . . strategy of identifying a mental state by appeal to a "content sentence", despite its utility in the workaday business of dealing with our fellow creatures, is simply out of place when our goal is the construction of a scientific theory about the mechanisms underlying behaviour' (Stich, 5–6). If Stich is right, radical cognitive psychology has a better prospect than behaviourism had of dislodging the interpretation of human action in terms of propositional attitudes. Unlike behaviourism, it has theoretically interesting things to say about the intellectual side of human life. And it does not dismiss the traditional approach as superstitious nonsense. Rather, it begins with traditional accounts of human action in terms of propositional attitudes, draws attention to specific defects in those accounts, and proposes revisions to remove those defects. While not traditional, it can plausibly claim to be a legitimate development of tradition.

Unlike the behaviourists, Stich is in two minds about the prospect he believes to be before us. For even if 'folk' accounts of human action cannot be incorporated into the explanatory cognitive psychology of the future, he foresees that they may remain practically indispensable (Stich, 213–14). Nor is he alone among philosophical advocates of psychology as a physical science in recognizing that the 'folk' conception of practical human behaviour in terms of propositional attitudes is also the conception that history and the social sciences have of it. K.V. Wilkes has well said that the 'conceptual apparatus' the 'folk' view analyses 'stands to that of scientific psychology as a multi-purpose tool stands to a spanner' (Wilkes, 150).

Unfortunately, many who acknowledge this contrive, like Berkeley, to persuade themselves that they can speak with the vulgar while they think with the learned. Thus Smart assures us that 'We need not devalue Gibbon's *Decline and Fall of the Roman Empire* because it uses language that is unsuitable for scientific purposes' – after all, 'What other language could a historian use?' (Smart, 176). Like Berkeley, they delude themselves. Of course there is nothing objectionable about speaking with the vulgar and thinking with the learned if the learned do not think that what the vulgar say is false. But that is exactly what the learned in question – those who have mastered radical cognitive psychology – do think about the vulgar language of propositional attitudes.

Nor will Quine's strategy of the double standard avail: the strategy of 'tolerat[ing] the idioms of propositional attitude' for practical purposes, as long as we forswear them when 'limning the true and ultimate structure of reality' (Quine (1), 221). Since historians claim to limn processes that truly occur in reality, we do not tolerate what they say if we deny its truth. By acknowledging that speech about propositional attitudes is characteristically causal, and only real entities can have causes and effects, Stich himself has implicitly conceded that the Quinean strategy would eliminate too much (cf. Stich, 244). If I believe as a matter of science that propositional attitudes are nonentities like phlogiston, then I contradict myself if I also accept as true history Gibbon's assertion that 'In the primitive church the influence of [Christians' confidence in immortality] was very powerfully strengthened by an opinion . . . which has not been found agreeable to experience . . . [namely,] that the end of the world, and the kingdom of heaven, were at hand.' If there are no propositional attitudes, then what Gibbon wrote is false in the most radical way possible: it ascribes to the primitive Christians not merely a property they did not have, but a property of a kind that nothing anywhere has ever had.

Moreover, jettisoning propositional attitudes would compromise the natural sciences as well as history. As R.G. Collingwood once observed, 'natural science as a form of thought exists and always has existed in a context of history' (Collingwood, 177). That is, all research in natural science depends on beliefs about the findings of others; and such beliefs do not differ in nature from historical beliefs in any field.

This can be verified by consulting any detailed history of a scientific discovery. J.D. Watson's narrative of the discovery of the helical structure of DNA abounds in examples. Here are some, from his description of his and Crick's reactions to the news that in Linus Pauling's latest model of the DNA molecule, which they feared might be correct, each phosphate group contained a bound hydrogen atom and so had no net charge.

> All our speculations about whether the divalent ions held the chains together would have made no sense if there were hydrogen atoms firmly bound to the phosphates.... When Francis [Crick] was amazed equally by Pauling's unorthodox chemistry, I began to breathe slower. By then, I knew we were still in the game.... The blooper was too unbelievable to keep secret for more than a few minutes. I dashed over to Roy Markham's lab to spurt out the news and to receive further confirmation that Linus' chemistry was screwy.... Next I hopped over to the organic chemists', where again I heard the soothing words that DNA was an acid (Watson, 103).

Watson here describes himself and Crick as reasonably believing two things about chemists generally: (1) that, for good scientific reasons, they both accepted certain principles about the nature of acids, and had concluded that DNA is an acid; and (2) that their principles and conclusion are inconsistent with Pauling's reported hypothesis that DNA's phosphate groups each contain a bound hydrogen atom and so have no net charge. He further describes himself as consulting other scientists to ascertain the truth of what he and Crick believed about their beliefs. Except in such a context of ascertainably shared belief, as Collingwood perceived, discoveries like Watson's and Crick's would be unthinkable.

Stich's own survey of the present state of cognitive psychology (or even Churchland's) shows that he too thinks of himself as working in just such a context. And one item from it has a moral. Some of the recent work which he judges 'not [to] comport comfortably with the folk psychological picture' has to do with cases of what is termed 'cognitive dissonance', in which the dissonance is between linguistic and non-linguistic behaviour (Stich, 235–7). But the concept was developed in connection with dissonant beliefs.

> The core idea of dissonance research [he writes] is that if subjects are led to behave in ways they find uncomfortable or unappealing and if they do not have what they take to be an adequate reason for enduring the effects of this behavior, then they will come to view the behavior or its effects as more attractive. . . . The explanation offered for the 'inadequate justification' phenomenon is that subjects note that they have done something they thought to be unpleasant without any adequate reason and explain this prima facie anomalous behavior with the hypothesis that the behavior or its consequences are not so unpleasant as they had thought (Stich, 232).

Nothing would be left of this passage if it were denied either that psychologists doing dissonance research both attribute beliefs to their subjects, and try to explain the beliefs they attribute to them; or that their colleagues and students in turn form beliefs about what those beliefs are. Nor would anything be left of Stich's argument that work in cognitive psychology could undermine the folk belief that much human behaviour is explained by human beings' propositional attitudes.

Churchland has objected that what he calls 'this very popular move' is question-begging; and he has fabricated a version of it that is indeed so, namely, 'that the thesis of eliminative materialism [i.e. that there are no such things as propositional attitudes at all] is incoherent since it denies the very conditions presupposed by the assumption that it is meaningful' (Churchland, 89). Far from dismissing as meaningless the denial that there are beliefs, the objection suggested by Collingwood's observation that natural science exists in a context of history accepts it as meaningful, and concludes that it contradicts the history of psychology as Churchland and Stich themselves tell it. It does not beg the question by assuming what they deny. Rather, it forbids them to consign to oblivion what, in making their case, they found it convenient to assert.

The thesis that there are no beliefs is perfectly intelligible; and so is the thesis that the belief that there are beliefs underlies a stagnant research programme. Both Churchland and Stich, in their different ways, assert the latter in arguing for the former. The objection is that it is inconsistent to do so. This objection may be unsound, but it begs no question. And on its face it is sound.

There is, as almost always in philosophy, a way out. If, along with a cognitive psychology that dispenses with propositional attitudes, successors to history and to practical discourse as we know them should also be developed, then a later Stich could write, in the new forms of discourse, a substitute for his brief history of cognitive psychology in *From Folk Psychology to Cognitive Science*. It would then become evident that

Collingwood had been wrong when he declared that natural science exists in a context of history. How wrong would depend on how much the successor to history in terms of which his substitute was written should turn out to differ from the history we know. If it should differ little, Collingwood would be substantially vindicated; for the tenor of Stich's predictions is that the revolutionary overthrow of folk psychology will be Copernican in magnitude.

One nightmare, however, can be put behind us. Stich foresees 'rough times' if, as he believes to be a serious possibility, our future cognitive science turns out to be inconsistent with the 'folk precepts that define who and what we are' (Stich, 10). The roughness will not endure long. If it is not accompanied by new forms of practical and historical discourse, revolutionary cognitive science will not survive, because it will be inconsistent with the context in which it must. And if it is so accompanied, it will be justified by new precepts defining who and what we are.

The condition of Churchland, Stich and their fellows is another matter. They have come to believe that the cognitive science in which they are engaged is (probably) incompatible with the existence of the propositional attitudes in terms of which they themselves understand science as a human activity. This is of far greater theoretical interest than the condition of the experimental subjects who, without having what they took to be adequate reason, were led to behave in ways they used to find unpleasant. As psychologists they take the position that there are no such things as propositional attitudes. On the other hand, as historians in the severe tradition of Acton, they denounce past psychologists for believing that much in human behaviour is explained by propositional attitudes like believing. Their findings as historians cannot appeal to them as psychologists.

The theory of cognitive dissonance, however, is confirmed. For, as predicted by that theory, when confronted with the fact that they do something unappealing, although they have good reason not to, they find doing it not so bad after all.

C.   Plan for an investigation of human action on Socratic lines

If the fundamental idea of the Socratic tradition is sound, that human actions are distinguished from the rest of human behaviour as being explained by their doers' propositional attitudes, any acceptable investigation of human action must be Socratic. However, the scope of such an investigation may well extend beyond human action. Human beings do not have at birth the capacity either to take propositional attitudes, or to govern their actions by those they take. Yet their nature is such that, with appropriate nurture and education, they will normally acquire both capacities. They are called 'rational animals' because of their capacity to acquire them. Now it may well be that other animals in the universe have this same capacity to acquire capacities. If the varieties of extra-terrestrial animals are numerous, then some presumably do have it. If any do, the theory of human action will also be the theory of their actions.

How is a contemporary Socratic investigation of the actions of human and other rational animals to be conducted? Although its fundamental idea has not generated programmes for research in psychology of the kinds Churchland and Stich desire, it has been fruitful. Aristotle, while following Socrates in explaining human actions by their doers' propositional attitudes, did not, as we have seen, explain them by the same attitudes. And, as we shall see, its progeny multiplied after Aristotle's death.

Any Socratic identification of human actions with doings explained by their doers' propositional attitudes may be interpreted differently according to the different opinions that are held about the ontological category to which doings belong. For brief periods, questions about such interpretations have dominated all others about action: philosophical journals in the early seventies gave the impression that the theory of action was a branch of the theory of categories. Accordingly, since it is well to eliminate categorial ambiguity, I begin in chapter 2 by arguing that doings, and hence actions, are a species of event; and that events are genuine individuals. Although propositional attitudes are states and not events, their comings to be and their persistences in being are events, like those of other states; and it is by their comings to be and their persistences that the events that are actions are explained.

The ground is now cleared for action theory proper. In chapter 3, I take as my working hypothesis Aristotle's doctrine that actions are events explained by their doers' choices, which are in turn explained by their wishes and beliefs. This is shown to imply that the propositional attitudes by which actions are explained are of two kinds, cognitive and appetitive, the appetitive ones being intellectual and not merely felt. The beliefs by which choices are derived from wishes are deliberative, and generate appetitive attitudes of an intermediate kind which the medieval Aristotelians called 'intentions'.

The process of deliberation or 'practical reasoning' raises a further problem. The reasonableness of any piece of such reasoning depends upon the reasonableness of the propositions to which the reasoner takes an attitude, and upon their logical relations; but neither, *prima facie*, determines what attitude the reasoner will take to them. Under what conditions, if any, does a sequence of propositional attitudes that would make a choice reasonable also explain it? This question cannot be answered until a number of others are.

The first of these other questions is semantical: how are utterances ascribing propositional attitudes to this person or that to be understood? In introducing the concept of a propositional attitude reference was made to propositions and to their constituents; and Frege's suggestion was briefly mentioned that they belong to a third world, collaboratively created by human beings in their linguistic communication, and distinct both from the spatio-temporal world of objects of sensation and feeling. Perhaps there is nothing ominous about this; but if propositions are entities in a third world, then until the truth-conditions of utterances about them have been systematically explained, we cannot expect to understand how their third-worldly logical relations can have any part in explaining the attitudes human beings take to them. This is attempted, on Fregean lines, in chapter 4.

The semantic clarifications of chapter 4 can now be applied, in chapter 5, to several problems that are sometimes taken to be fatal to the Socratic tradition itself. They at once dissipate the fog enveloping the well-known fact that attitudes to propositions about individual objects and events in the world are about those objects and events only 'under certain descriptions'. But there is a more difficult problem. To any Socratic definition of actions as doings explained by their doers' taking attitudes to propositions about them it appears that there are counterexamples, and that they can be excluded only if in those propositions the doings explained are described, with epistemic circularity, as actions. Against this, it is argued that they can be excluded without such circularity if in each such proposition the doing in question is described as explained by the attitude that is being taken to it. This done, the version of the medieval Aristotelian action theory outlined in chapter 3 has been elucidated and shown to be defensible.

Two principal tasks remain with respect to it. The first, carried out in chapter 6, is to give some idea of how it is now being developed, by investigating the implications of the character of intentions as plans. An asymmetry between the attitudes of believing and intending underlies some of this development. The second, carried out in chapter 7, is to take

up the continuing controversy about how explanations of
actions by their doers' propositional attitudes are themselves
to be understood. They are obviously not physical, and some
have maintained that they are not causal either: that they are,
in fact, explanations of the kind Anaxagoras inspired Socrates
to demand – explanations in terms of what it is reasonable to
do, or for the best. Since some who are convinced of this are
our friends, as Aristotle said of the Platonists, I regretfully
argue that they are mistaken, and that explanations of actions
by their doers' propositional attitudes are causal. Our action
theory proper is now complete.

What does it imply about who and what we are? First of all,
that we are creatures not merely of desire, but also of will. It is
argued in chapter 8 that an acceptable theory of intention
must show that human action can be explained neither in
terms of beliefs and felt desires alone (a view which allows
human beings intellectual cognitive attitudes, but not intellectual appetites), nor by treating a certain variety of belief as
appetitive (reviving the original Socratic idea that action is
explained by cognitive attitudes alone). The concept of will
cannot be relegated to the museum of obsolete scientific ideas,
along with those of the luminiferous ether and the Freudian
death-wish. And secondly, it implies that will is a general
power to choose intellectual appetitive attitudes, whether they
be choices to do now what you believe to be in your power, or
wishes, or intentions. In addition, it is argued in chapter 9, this
general power is of a kind which its possessors may exercise or
not, unlike the power of fire to burn or of water to quench.
Objections to the very concept of such a power are considered,
some of them generated by the notion of 'agent causation',
which should be avoided as paradoxical to contemporary ears,
even though it is historically defensible.

Anybody constructing, or reconstructing, a theory in which
the central element in the explanation of human action is the
exercise of this general power of choice, unfortunately puts

himself in a position in which it would be discreditable to say nothing about the barren question, 'Are human beings free in exercising their power to choose?' What I have to say about it in chapter 10 will presumably persuade nobody, although many will think it true but not new – indeed, obviously true.

CHAPTER 2

ACTIONS AS INDIVIDUAL EVENTS

Human actions are those human doings that can be explained by their doers' propositional attitudes. But what are doings? Although the examples so far considered have all been bits of bodily behaviour, not all doings are. Human beings make calculations not only on their fingers and on paper, but also in their heads; and the latter are as good specimens of full human actions as the former. Yet it is convenient to begin with bodily doings. Since they are easier to study than mental ones, it is reasonable to suppose that it will be easier to construct a theory of them, and to extend it to what we do in our heads, than to construct from the beginning a theory covering both.

What is it for one bit of bodily behaviour to be the same as another or different from it? A philosopher who cannot tell us what it is for Phormio's tripping Geta to be the same as the funny bit of behaviour that happened on the way to the forum, or to be different from it, does not know what a bit of behaviour is, and hence is not entitled to tell us that bodily human actions are a species of bits of behaviour.

Everybody knows what it is for the dog that was put out last night to be the same as the dog on the doorstep in the morning, even though many of us are quite unable to put that knowledge into words. Yet knowing what it is for animals to be the same or not must be distinguished from knowing how to tell whether they are the same or not. Everybody knows what it is for sheep to be the same, though shepherds with large flocks may have no way of telling whether the sheep that strayed yesterday is the same as the sheep that is lagging today. Just as zoologists must be able to put into words what the first of these two pieces of knowledge is, and to give advice about how to arrange that the second should be or be made obtainable, so philosophers may be expected to put into words what it is for one bit of behaviour to be the same as another or different from it, and to give advice about how to arrange matters so that we can tell whether one such bit is or is not the same as another.

Philosophers are largely agreed that doings are events (or happenings, or occurrences); but they are far from agreed about what events are. It is sometimes assumed that all events are changes. That is certainly a mistake. Socrates' staying in prison was an event that was also an action, a refraining from the escape his friends had arranged; but it was not a change. Nor need such a refraining be from bringing about some specific change. In a bad situation, not 'doing something' when there is nothing to be done is also an action, as Milton implicitly recognized when he comforted himself with the thought that

They also serve, who only stand and wait.

It is true that colloquial usage permits us to deny that non-happenings of changes are events: to say that a dog's doing nothing in the night-time is not an incident, and to disparage standing and waiting as inaction. But it also permits us to follow the good example of Conan Doyle's Sherlock Holmes, and describe the persistence of a state of something as an incident – an event – as well as a change in one.

States, as states are here understood, are a subspecies of properties or attributes. Not all properties are states. A state is a property a thing can have for a time, and hence can come to have or cease to have. The number four has the property of being even, but it is not in a state of evenness; and a sphere has the property of having all points on its surface equidistant from a given point, but it is not in a state of having them so. On the other hand, a balloon when inflated can come to be in a spherical state, and can cease to be in that state when it is deflated. Although there is nothing logically improper in it, it is unusual to describe having a simple property, such as a colour, as being in a state; for a state is normally thought of as the property of having parts having certain properties, often relational ones. Hence only bodies of stuff (the pond) and complex things (the living room) are as a rule described as being in states (of calm, of readiness for a party).

Philosophical disagreement arises because such events as the persistence of the pond in a state of calm for a time, and its later coming to be in a state of roughness, are at first glance indistinguishable from the pair of facts or states of affairs that it is calm for a time and that later it comes to be rough. And some philosophers, like Wittgenstein when he wrote his *Tractatus*, believe that facts are entities depicted by such sentences as 'The pond is calm' and 'The pond has become rough'. And they further believe that the existence or nonexistence of those entities determines the truth of the sentences depicting them. They therefore think of the world as made up of facts.

Two widely received philosophical theories of action, Chisholm's and Alvin Goldman's, follow lines of thought parallel to Wittgenstein's. Chisholm's, the more complex, identifies events with a subspecies of states of affairs, and states of affairs with what somebody can possibly accept as true; and declares two states of affairs to be the same if each entails the other (Chisholm (1), 117–18). Goldman's theory identifies events with what he calls property-exemplifications: two events are the same if they are exemplifications of the same property by the same individual object at the same time (Goldman, 10–13, 172). Actions are events in which the individual object is a person, and the exemplification of the property arises from propositional attitudes of that person.

If events are entities like facts, as Chisholm and Goldman believe, then they proliferate. For, as Goldman has pointed out, generalizing and adapting an observation first made by G.E.M. Anscombe (Anscombe (1), 37–40), every fact of change or persistence necessarily generates numerous others. This is best shown by an example. Consider the putative fact/event:

(1) The pond remained calm throughout 26 May 1985.

Let us suppose that the following non-events are also facts:

(2) The pond's being calm invariably moves its oldest inhabitant to take his boat out

(a matter of cause and effect);

(3) Whitsunday in 1985 falls on the 26th May,

and

(4) By a local ordinance, children under ten may swim in the pond only when it is calm

(matters of convention); and finally,

(5) The 26th was the only day in May on which I was away from the pond

(a matter of non-conventional circumstance).

Given the facts (2)–(5) – their particular character does not matter, because similar results would follow for any others – the fact/event that the pond was calm on 26 May 1985 begets the following further facts/events about the pond:

(6) The state of the pond throughout 26 May 1985 was such as to move its oldest inhabitant to go boating (out of (2))
(7) The pond remained calm throughout Whitsunday, 1985 (out of (3))
(8) The state of the pond throughout 26 May 1985 was such

that children under ten were legally permitted to swim in it (out of (4)),

(9) The pond remained calm throughout the only day in May when I was away from it (out of (5)).

And these in turn beget others. For example,

(10) The state of the pond throughout Whitsunday, 1985, was such that children under ten were legally permitted to swim in it (out of (3) and (8)).

If events are entities like facts, this fecundity is inescapable. It may even appear to be unobjectionable. We do not object to the fecundity by which every true proposition p generates an infinity of others: p, it is true that p, it is true that it is true that p, and so on. Yet there is a difference between the two cases. Truths are propositions, and as such belong to what Frege thought of as the third world: the world of objects of thought (Frege (2), 68–77/362–72). There is no difficulty at all in supposing that thought is such that for every truth about something it is possible to construct an infinity of other equivalent truths. But events are happenings or occurrences in the world; and different ways of thinking about them can no more add to their number than taking thought can add a cubit to our stature. On both Goldman's and Chisholm's accounts of event/fact identity, none of the events/facts (6)–(9) is identical with the pair of facts, one an event and the other not, that generates it. Each is a different exemplification from either member of that pair, and the pair itself is not an exemplification. And although the pair entail it, it does not entail the pair. Yet once the generating event/fact (1) has happened, nothing more need happen for the generated event/fact to happen: all that is necessary is that certain other facts that are not events be the case.

That, however, seems false. If a certain happening is distinct from another, then something more than that other must happen if it is to happen. And this condition is not met in two of the kinds of event/fact in Goldman's classification: those simply generated, and those conventionally generated. In the former, one event generates another given no more than that it happens in certain circumstances other than the obtaining of a convention; in the latter, it does so given that a convention obtains. But it may seem that what he calls causal generation, exemplified in the generation of (6) by (1) out of (2), is another matter. For it may seem that (6) cannot be the case until something has happened besides (1), namely:

(11) The oldest inhabitant has gone boating.

That, however, is a mistake.

The oldest inhabitant's having gone boating is indeed an event distinct from the pond's having remained calm throughout the day; but it is also an event distinct from the pond's being such as to move him to go boating. His boating is neither identical with nor part of any event that caused it. The event narrated in (6) is the persistence of the pond in a certain state, identified by reference to its effect on the oldest inhabitant; and its effect, narrated in (11), is neither identical with it nor a part of it. As Davidson has pointed out, it is a mistake to think 'that when the description of an event is made to include reference to a consequence, then the consequence itself is included in the described event' (Davidson (1), 58).

As for the oldest inhabitant's having been moved to go boating, it is not an event at all. It is true that definite descriptions of events can be formed by nominalizing sentences narrating them. But, since not every sentence narrates an event, not every nominalization of a sentence describes one. The nominalization 'The oldest inhabitant's having been moved to go boating' is a case in point. The sentence it normalizes (namely, 'The oldest inhabitant was moved to go boating') does not narrate an event, but expresses the proposition that a certain event (the oldest inhabitant's going boating) had a cause. Presumably most events, if not all, have causes;

but the truth that a given event has a cause is not a truth about a third event distinct from both that event and its cause.

Goldman vainly attempts to dispose of this objection by grouping events into 'event-trees', and treating distinct events as distinct occurrences only when they belong to distinct event-trees. Events belonging to the same event-tree are related by what he calls 'level-generation'. Roughly, an event 'level-generates' another if, given its circumstance and causality but not otherwise, its occurrence entails, mediately or immediately, the occurrence of that other. (An exact definition of act-generation is given in Goldman, 43: I have generalized it for events.) An event that is not itself level-generated, and the complete set of events it level-generates, in the logical order in which they follow from it, together constitute an event-tree. Nothing but the level-generating event need occur for the whole of the tree it generates to occur; but for an event outside that tree to occur something else must. The objection to this is that no philosophical reason has been given (other than to save a theory) for discriminating the concept of an event from that of a happening or occurrence.

Goldman's distinction is even less persuasive when applied to events that are bringings about of changes. After performing one such feat, nobody would be credited with performing another, as Irving Thalberg has pointed out, unless it called for some exertion besides that constituting the first (Thalberg (1), 105–7). When Leon Czolgosz shot President McKinley on 6 September 1901, his action was not believed to be murder, because the President was expected to live. That it was a murder became known eight days later, when the President died. Czolgosz, having shot the President, did nothing more to murder him. He did not need to. He harmlessly spent the whole interval between the shooting and the death in custody. The shooting and the death were two distinct events, but the shooting and the murder were not. This is recognized by the criminal law, according to which, while the shooting and the death have different dates, the shooting and the murder do not (cf. Davidson (1), 177–8; Aune, 12–16).

Yet if not all actions are bringings about of changes, as has been argued above, Thalberg's reasoning has a lacuna. If standing and waiting can be an action, why should not Czolgosz's waiting in custody be one? Implicitly, the answer was anticipated by Socrates: standing and waiting is an action only when it is chosen in preference to bringing about a change within one's power. If, after shooting him, Czolgosz could have done something that would have saved the President's life, but instead stood and waited, then his idleness would have been a further action: indeed, in some cases it would have been the murder, not the shooting.

Amending Thalberg's argument to allow for actions that are not bringings about of changes, it would run: actions are distinct from one another if and only if they are bringings about of change calling for distinct exertions, or are refrainings from such energetic bringings about. By this test, the distinct facts constituting one of Goldman's action-trees are not actions. No facts are.

Wittgenstein (in his *Tractatus* phase) and Russell (in his logical atomist phase) believed that the world is made up of facts, because they were convinced that propositions depict facts, and are true or false according as the facts they depict exist or do not, that is, according as they 'correspond to' facts or do not. Against this, Frege argued that to identify truth with a relation between propositions and something else is incompatible with the necessity of the equivalence principle that distinguishes the truth-predicate from all others: namely, that the result of adding the operator 'It is true that' to a true or false sentence is a new sentence having the same truth-value as the one to which it was added (Frege (2), 62-3/355–6; cf. Dummett (1), 442–6, 463–4). But if truth is not a relation between propositions and facts, then Wittgenstein's and Russell's reason for recognizing facts as entities distinct from true propositons vanishes. Whether a given proposition is true depends on what entities there are in the world, but not on whether it depicts or mirrors those entities. It is true that some roses are red if and only if red roses are among the entities composing the world; but the sentence expressing that proposition does not depict or mirror red roses. In the same way, it is true that Socrates remained in prison by choice if and only if his waiting for death (an event that is an action) was among the entities composing the world; but again, the sentence expressing that proposition does not depict or mirror his waiting.

It would be ridiculous to pretend that semantical positions like Chisholm's and Goldman's can be demolished by briefly outlining Frege's argument against the correspondence theory, and his realist alternative to postulating that the world is made up of facts. Not only is semantics in the tradition of logical atomism still persuasively defended (see, e.g. Hochberg, 271–308, 414–43), but newer theories are in the field. Castaneda's has already been mentioned. An even more recent one, deriving from first order model theory, postulates the existence of something very like facts, namely, situations (Barwise and Perry, 7–26). Why, then, cleave to the Fregean semantical tradition? Out of prudence. Action theory is not the only branch of philosophy in which semantical questions cannot be avoided; and in all such branches investigators must choose between a variety of approaches. I have chosen the Fregean one because it is the most fully elaborated, and because it remains defensible. Even if it turns out to be wrong, it has been developed so far that, provided that no other errors have been made, results obtained by following it may be expected both to approximate the truth and to be readily corrigible.

Within the Fregean tradition, the semantic function of a sentence is to express a truth or a falsehood, not to refer to any of the objects that compose the world. (Frege himself held that they name one or other of the truth-values, the True and the

False, which he recognized as objects; but there is no need to follow him in this – cf. Dummett (1), 182–3.) The individual objects that compose the world are referred to by the parts of true sentences that stand for what those sentences are about: namely, names or definite descriptions. Many sentences, it is true, contain neither, but that is because they are general, and so not about particular individual objects (cf. Davidson (1), 168–72). In both the classical and the modern European languages, while events are seldom if ever given proper names, definite descriptions of them abound: for example, 'the trial of Socrates', 'the Reformation', 'the funny thing that happened on the way to the forum'.

Within the Fregean tradition, that a definite description forms part of a true sentence affords no more than a presumption that it stands for an object in the world. Many such sentences can, without altering their meaning, be so rephrased that the definite descriptions they contain vanish. And when such rephrasing accords with the semantic theory the tradition provides, the presumption that those descriptions stand for objects in the world also vanishes. Some philosophers working on Fregean lines, among whom P.T. Geach is conspicuous, have maintained that all true sentences that contain definite descriptions of events can be acceptably rephrased to eliminate them. His argument runs as follows:

> 'Queen Anne's death is a past event' goes over into 'Queen Anne has died' (or 'is dead'), and 'The news of Queen Anne's death made Lord Bolingbroke swear' goes over into 'Lord Bolingbroke swore because he heard Queen Anne had died.' . . .[I]n this way, we get a manner of speaking in which persons and things are mentioned but events do not even appear to be mentioned; so far from its being people and things that are logical constructions out of events, events are logical constructions out of people and things (Geach (2), 313).

Such a strategy will without doubt eliminate most of the

definite descriptions of events that occur in true sentences about them. Does it, as Geach contends, eliminate all?

F.I. Dretske was among the first to draw attention to the difficulty of eliminating them from sentences about when an event occurs, for example, 'The battle of Ramillies was fought in 1706' (Dretske, 481–4; cf. Davidson (1), 170*n*.). On the face of it, this sentence says that a certain individual, a battle, stands in a certain relation (namely, that of occurring at an interval within it) to a certain period of time. It is possible, by rephrasing it roughly, to eliminate the definite description 'the battle of Ramillies': for example, by writing 'In 1706, once and only once, some armies joined battle at Ramillies.' But not only does the rephrased sentence, although true, not render the sense of the original exactly (many places after which battles are named are not those where they were fought), it obscures its logical structure.

What does 'in' stand for in 'In 1706, once and only once, armies joined battle at Ramillies'? If it is for the relation something has to a temporal interval within which it occurs, and I know of no defensible semantics according to which it stands for anything else, then what things is that relation said to relate? One is the year 1706: namely, the interval within which the other is said to have occurred. What is the other? It cannot be the armies that joined battle, because the relation of occurring within relates temporal intervals to relata that are datable. Events are datable, but the continuing things to which they happen are not. To rephrase a sentence containing a dyadic relational predicate in such a way as to eliminate explicit reference to either of its relata is objectionable according to any defensible semantics. Yet that is done by the proposed rephrasing of 'The battle of Ramillies was fought in 1706'. And the ineliminable relational predicate 'in' dumbly testifies that reference to the battle has been eliminated only in appearance. It remains implicit.

Reference to events is a semantic necessity if continuing and hence undatable individual objects are to relate to time at all. Whether an individual is a person, an army, or an inanimate parcel of solid, fluid or gaseous stuff, it relates to time by entering into events. This becomes evident as soon as the sentences in which such relations are stated are put into a form in which the relata of those relations are explicitly referred to.

That most narratives of events in colloquial speech conceal that they refer to events should not disturb anybody. The quantificational structure of colloquial speech is so unperspicuous that an adequate theory of it is barely a century old. As Wittgenstein observed in his *Tractatus*,

> Language disguises thought. So much so that from the outward form of the clothing it is impossible to infer the form of the thought beneath it – the tacit conventions on which the understanding of everyday thought depends are extremely complicated (Wittgenstein (1), 4.002).

If events are individuals, they will not be expressly referred to in most sentences that narrate them, but only in definite descriptions corresponding to some of those sentences.

And that is not all. If events are individuals, like physical objects and persons, not merely one, but a multitude of definite descriptions will be true of each of them, as of every individual. Certain of the sentences narrating them will be transformable, wholly or in part, into each definite description. And for each of Goldman's event trees and action trees there will be a tree of definite descriptions of an individual event or an individual action. This is the position taken by Anscombe (Anscombe (1), 45–7) and Davidson (Davidson (1), 169–80).

To illustrate it by a classical example. In Sophocles' *Oedipus Rex* (801–12), Oedipus tells Jocasta that, just before he became king, he had met, at the crossroads of Phocis, an old man in a carriage, attended by five servants. When they tried to push him off the road, he became angry and struck the coachman, whereupon the old man hit him on the head with his goad.

Infuriated, he struck the old man backwards out of the carriage with his stick, so that he fell dead in the road. Then he killed all the attendants, except one who made off. Later, the attendant who escaped gives evidence that the old man in the carriage was Laius, Oedipus' father.

Although Oedipus does not give definite descriptions of any of the actions he narrates, such descriptions are easily constructed from Sophocles' text. One would be: 'Oedipus' striking of Laius with his stick.' Given its effect, the action thus described can also be truly described as 'Oedipus' killing of Laius.' And given the circumstance that Laius was Oedipus' father, it can further be truly described as 'Oedipus' killing of his father.' Each of these descriptions corresponds to what Goldman would recognize as a distinct level generated action. However, if actions are individual entities, there is only one action which all three describe, each in a different way: one by referring to a fairly immediate effect (that it resulted in Laius' being struck by the stick), one by referring to a more remote effect (that Laius died of it), and one by referring both to that more remote effect and to a circumstance – that Oedipus and Laius were related in a certain way (being son and father).

Even if continuing individual objects can be linguistically represented in relation to time only by referring to events in which they are implicated, it is possible to doubt whether events are really part of the furniture of the world. For it is possible to suspect that natural languages are in various respects radically misleading. One ground for suspecting it is that, while individual events are referred to by definite descriptions, it is not clear what it would be for them to be the same or not the same. If it is logically defensible to use two given definite descriptions at all, then the question whether or not they refer to the same thing must always have a true answer. Does it, when the things two such descriptions refer to are events? For example, it is the concept of a change in the state of an object such that there is always a true answer to the question whether the change of a from the state F to the state G during the interval from t_1 to t_2 is or is not the same as the change of b from F_1 to G_1 during that same interval? The question is not whether such answers can always be found (presumably if there always is one then sometimes it cannot), but whether they are there to be found. If we have no reason to believe that they are, then we have reason to suspect that the concept of an event is radically flawed.

Fewer questions can be answered than we should like about whether different definite descriptions do or do not describe the same event. Yet it is easy to show that events do not differ in this respect from other kinds of individual, say, physical objects. If an event is a change or a persistence in a state (i.e. a property) of some set of objects (perhaps a set having only one member), then sometimes the identity conditions for events can be specified wholly in terms of the identity conditions of the sets of objects and the intervals of time in which they occur: namely, when the properties in the persistence or change of which they consist are specified in the same way in both descriptions.

Is the changing of a, between 7.00 and 7.05 p.m. Eastern Standard Time, from being F to being G the same as the changing of b, between 4.00 and 4.05 p.m. Pacific Standard Time, from being F to being G? Well, is a the same as b? If a and b are physical objects it is not seriously disputed that this question has a true answer. Does the change in a occur in the same interval of time as the change in b? Here too, it is not seriously disputed that the question whether a given time according to Eastern Standard is or is not the same as a time according to Pacific Standard has a true answer. And in the two descriptions sketched, since the state in the changing of which the event described consists is specified in the same way, no question arises about whether or not the same state is described. Hence there are event descriptions about which it is not seriously disputed that the question whether they do or do not describe the same events has a true answer. It is simply not true that identity conditions for events cannot be given.

Some purported definite descriptions of events fail to be so because they fail to identify the set of individual objects in which or to which the events they purport to describe happen; but it follows neither that there are no such events, nor that definite descriptions of them cannot be given. However, a *prima facie* case can be made for suspecting that describing events by referring to their effects or circumstances raises insoluble identity problems; and if that suspicion is confirmed, the sense of sentences containing such descriptions would become suspect also.

In our example from Sophocles, Oedipus implicitly describes one of his actions as a change in himself that resulted in an insolent stranger's being killed, and Laius' surviving attendant implicitly describes an action he witnessed as a change in an unknown man that resulted in the killing of Laius. Do these two descriptions describe the same change? As in most narratives of action, each description is indirect, by way of an effect of the change it describes. Neither specifies the state involved in the change it describes. But in the absence of such a specification, how can it be known whether or not those descriptions describe the same change?

This difficulty also vanishes on closer scrutiny. Specific properties can be referred to indirectly, for example, either as generic properties of some identified individual at a certain time (e.g. as 'being the colour of your grandfather's last car when he bought it') or as a properties the coming to be or persistence of which in some individual has a specified effect (e.g. as 'being the colour the signal light has changed to, thereby causing you to brake'). And sometimes it can be known that properties thus indirectly referred to are the same: that when your grandfather bought his last car it was red, the same colour as the signal light changed to when it caused you to brake.

Sophocles' dramatic presentation of the evidence of how Laius was killed shows how different indirect descriptions can refer to a change of the same properties of the same individual. First, Oedipus himself testifies that, on a certain date, he met one and only one old man in a carriage at the crossroads of Phocis, that he struck him with his stick, as a result of which the old man died. The surviving attendant testifies that the old man in the carriage who was killed on that date at the crossroads of Phocis was Laius. It is not questioned in the play that all speak the truth. And if they do, it follows that one and the same change of Oedipus' state, whatever that state may have been, was: (i) his striking of that old man with his stick, (ii) his striking of Laius with his stick, and (iii) his causing of Laius' death, that is (iv) his killing of Laius. It is true that we do not know exactly which of Oedipus' states (which set of his properties) that change involved: for example, whether it involved the positions of one or both of his hands, or whether whatever movements of his hands it involved were more up and down, or more sideways. But we know enough. Whatever change of his properties his action consisted in, it was the killing of Laius.

Although Sophocles' tragedy is not history, it accurately represents how courts establish whether the things different witnesses testify about actions are or are not about the same action. Once that is understood, action theorists can forget the philosophers' stone they have vainly sought, namely, a principle of individuation for actions. They do not need it. As Davidson has remarked, 'we make good enough sense of assertions and denials of identity' about many kinds of thing, even though there are no good formulas for identifying them (Davidson (1), 180).

The ultimate genus of bodily actions is that of events. Events are individual objects of a special kind: namely, changes or persistences in states of continuing individual objects. They are represented linguistically, as other individuals are, by individual names or definite descriptions, and not by sentences. More specifically, bodily actions are bits of bodily behaviour, that is events in animal bodies arising out of sensation or thinking. But not all such bits of bodily behaviour are actions of the kind that is characteristic of human beings. Those that are can be explained by reference to the propositional attitudes of the animals of whose history they are part.

Extending this analysis to mental operations is not difficult. Doings that occur in the minds of animals, such as calculations, are doings just as much as bits of bodily behaviour. And they have the same genus: namely, they are events. Not all doings in the head are full human actions. Involuntary and undirected imaging is not. But some are: namely, those that, like bodily actions, are explained by the propositional attitudes of the animal in whose head they are done.

What of the propositional attitudes by which some of the events occurring in animal bodies and minds are explained? Are they events too? Strictly, no. Having a mental attitude, like being in a physical posture, is being in a state (cf. Kenny (2), 53, 120); and being in a state is a property or attribute. But coming to have a mental attitude you did not have before is a change of state, and so an event; and continuing in a mental attitude you have come to have is a persistence in a state, and so also an event. Propositional attitudes explain human actions because human beings come to have them and sometimes persist in them. They are not events, but they explain human actions by way of events.

CHAPTER 3

OREXIS AND *DOXA*

The propositional attitude by which Socrates explained his remaining in prison was a belief (*doxa*): the belief that to do so would be for the best. Aristotle ventured a correction. Socrates remained in prison because he chose to; but he 'can hardly be said' to have believed to (cf. Aristotle (4), III, 1112a 4–5). Since no belief is necessarily acted on, actions cannot be explained solely by their agents' beliefs. Propositional attitudes of some other kind must be at work: attitudes the natural behavioural expression of which is trying to bring about (cf. Anscombe (1), 68). Aristotle's generic term for such attitudes was '*orexis*', which the medieval Aristotelians rendered into Latin as '*appetitus*'. In revising the Oxford translation of Aristotle, Jonathan Barnes has followed their example, rendering it as 'appetite'.

According to Aristotle, action originates when an intellectual appetitive attitude of wishing that some end (*telos*) be brought about gives rise to deliberation (*bouleusis*) about how to bring it about. Deliberating how to bring it about that Athens be harmed by him as little as possible, Socrates concluded that by remaining in prison he could harm Athens less than by any other course of action open to him. His conclusion in turn generated a deliberative (and so derivative) *orexis* to remain there. And that derivative *orexis*, which Aristotle called a '*prohairesis*', or choice, is what directly explains his action.

The elements by which Aristotle held that human action is to be explained are therefore three: wishing for an end (*boulesis*); believing, as a result of deliberation, that a certain kind of action in one's power would effectively serve to bring about that end (*doxa*, resulting from *bouleusis*); and, as a result of these, choosing an action of that kind (*prohairesis*). All three, of course, are propositional attitudes: the first and third being orectic or appetitive, and the second cognitive.

Just as human actions are events in the world, whether bits of physical behaviour, or mental operations like calculations or resolutions, so are the changes or persistences in propositional attitudes – both *orexes* and *doxai* – by which they are explained. Changes and persistences in propositional attitudes are not themselves human actions; for to suppose that they are would generate vicious infinite regresses. Rather, they are 'acts' (*energeiai*) in the sense of actualizations of human potentialities. Of any of your appetites or beliefs it may be asked, 'When did you come to have it?' and 'How long did you stick to it?' Coming to have a propositional attitude is a process, often an active one; but persisting in one is not. You cannot be continuously believing the Nicene Creed, or be continuously wishing to be saved from damnation. But you can continue to believe in the one and to wish for the other. This is not a peculiarity of mental events. Persistences of physical states are events, but they neither are processes nor necessarily involve them. (Cf. Geach (1), 1–10; Kenny (1), 203–11; Sellars (2), 47–51.)

The principal question the Aristotelian scheme of explanation raises is: in what sense do actions 'result' from their agents' choices, or their choices from their wishes for ends and their beliefs that things they can do will bring those ends about? It can be answered only by exploring further the propositional attitudes that have these 'results'.

Anscombe has rightly insisted that *orexis* (which she renders as 'wanting') is not the same thing as desire – or appetite for what is felt as attractive (for which Aristotle's word was '*epithumia*'). Because desire is an attraction that can be *felt*, Anscombe speaks of 'the prick of desire at the thought or sight of an object, even though a man then does nothing towards getting the object' (Anscombe (1), 67). *Orexis*, or appetite, is the genus, of which the species are: on one side, desire, which is felt; and, on the other, wishing for an end and choosing an action for the sake of an end, which are not felt, although they sometimes have effects that are (cf. Aristotle (2) III, 433a 22–6).

The behaviour of animals lacking intellect is caused by desires operating on what they sense and imagine. They can have no appetites other than desires; and their behaviour at any time is therefore a matter of what they most strongly desire among what at that time they sense or imagine as possible. By contrast, animals possessed of intellect, like human beings, have intellectual appetites as well as felt ones, and their actions are normally to be explained by them. While they have desires, or felt appetites, for the most part they are moved by their desires only by way of the appetites of wishing and choosing, which are not felt. That they desire to bring about something will normally explain what they do only if they wish to bring about what they desire, and choose to do what they do in order to bring it about.

The appetites of wishing and choosing are intellectual in two respects. First, the only objects to which they are directed are thought of, and not merely sensed or imagined. Secondly, as attitudes to those objects they are not felt: they stand to desires as thinking of something pleasant to taste stands to tasting it. You may desire to do something you think of, but you cannot wish or choose to do something you imagine, unless you also think of it. And you may wish or choose to do not only what you desire to do, but also what you feel no attraction at all to doing. Too many have been disillusioned, like John Stuart Mill, by discovering that they would feel no joy in the attainment of the great ends they were brought up to wish for – whether the greatest happiness of the greatest number or a new birth of freedom. Only some, like him, are fortunate enough to discover that they can continue to wish for those ends nevertheless. Aristotle had no word for the specific intellectual *orexis* of which wish and choice are subspecies. The Latin Aristotelians did: the word '*voluntas*', which has gone into English as 'will'. Hence they rightly extended Aristotle's description of choice as '*orexis dianoetike*' or 'rational appetite' to the whole species of which it is a variety, and defined '*voluntas*' as rational appetite.

What happens when an agent deliberates and chooses? The few examples Aristotle discusses, while endearingly quaint (Aristotle (4) VII, 1147a 4–9; (2) 701a8–b1), are less enlightening than his description of deliberation:

> a doctor does not deliberate whether he shall heal, . . . nor does anyone else deliberate about his end. Having set the end they consider how and by what means it is to be attained; and if it seems to be produced by several means they consider by which it is most easily and best produced, while if it is achieved by one only they consider how it will be achieved by this and by what means *this* will be achieved, till they come to the first cause, which in the order of discovery is the last. For the person who deliberates seems to inquire and analyse in the way described as though he were analysing a geometrical construction . . . and what is last in the order of analysis seems to be the first in the order of becoming (Aristotle (4) III, 1112b 12–24).

Practical deliberation begins with a prospective agent wishing for an end, that is, wishing for some event to be brought about, and believing that it may be in his power to bring it about. The practical question about which he deliberates is: What kind of action (or series of actions) in his power will bring about (or be the first step in bringing about) the end he wishes for? And the important thing about this question is that he may rightly deem it answered as soon as he finds a way to work the trick that is in his power.

It does not matter if it can be worked in other ways, any more than it matters in solving a problem in geometrical construction. Of course, if several ways of working it occur to him, he will naturally inquire which most completely meets his other wishes. But, unless what he wishes for is, say, the neatest or cheapest solution to a problem he knows to have many solutions, the conclusion of his deliberation will not be the one and only thing it is practically reasonable to do.

Nor will it be a thing it is always reasonable for him to do. Deliberation is about things wished for; and there are some things (for example, breakfast) it is reasonable to wish for early in the morning, but not at mid-afternoon.

Aristotle's examples of practical reasoning are often misinterpreted because these implications of his description of deliberation are neglected. Yet there is a reason why they are neglected. He introduces the concepts of wish and deliberation in the course of showing how choice is to be explained. But choosing to do something, say, to fry yourself some bacon and eggs, is distinct both from not choosing to do anything and from choosing to do anything else you might do instead. So an adequate explanation of your choosing to fry yourself bacon and eggs must entail that you neither omit to choose to do anything nor choose to do something else. In technical terms, the *explanandum* must be deducible from the *explanans*. And that seems to require that the explanation must show that your wishes are of such a kind, and your deliberations are of such a kind, that anybody having wishes of that kind, and having carried out deliberations of that kind, must choose as you did. In other words, if practical reasoning is to explain action, its premises must be universal, and its individual conclusion must be a case falling under a universal conclusion that follows deductively. But so interpreted, as Anscombe has pointed out, Aristotelian practical reasoning is insane (Anscombe (1), 61);

and Bruce Aune has shown that recent attempts to make it sane by formalizing it differently are implausible (Aune, 117–37, 144–97; cf. Sellars (1), 110–13, 117–39).

Consider a simple example of Aristotelian practical reasoning. Dr John H. Watson ruminates:

A. (1) Can I make myself a good breakfast?
   (2) Well, fried bacon and eggs would be a good one;
   (3) and, how jolly! bacon and eggs are in the larder.
   (4) So, I'll fry myself some.

According to the insane interpretation, nobody whose choice is explained by his wish to make himself a good breakfast, and by his belief that fried bacon and eggs are a good breakfast and are available, can have that wish and those beliefs without choosing to act on them. Hence everybody having like wishes and like beliefs must always be choosing to fry himself bacon and eggs. True, that is insane; but how can Watson's deliberation explain why he chooses to fry himself bacon and eggs, as distinct from choosing something else or nothing at all, except on that plainly insane interpretation? Weaken any of the premises thus insanely interpreted, and it appears that it will cease to follow that he chooses as he does.

The grounds of this dilemma are plain. As Aristotle describes them, processes of deliberation like our apocryphal Watson's are attempts to answer, not questions of the form, 'What must you do that will bring about such and such, which you wish?' but rather those of the form, 'What can you do that will bring it about?' Yet there are two objections to the claim he goes on to make: that your belief that you can, in a certain way, bring about such and such, which you wish, explains why you choose to bring it about in that way. The first is that, since you may have other wishes, and may not be able to gratify them all, that you believe that a wish you have can be gratified in a certain way cannot explain why you choose to gratify it. And the second difficulty is that, even supposing that you will choose to gratify a certain wish if you believe that it can be gratified in a certain way, that you believe it does not explain why you choose that way of gratifying it, because you may believe that it can be gratified in other ways.

A second look at Aristotle's description of deliberation disposes of both these difficulties. The first depends on the false assumption that you deliberate whenever you form beliefs about how some wish you have *might be* gratified. Deliberation is practical reflection on how *to* gratify a given wish; and engaging in it presupposes that you think of the wish that generates it as one to be gratified. Human beings wish for a variety of things while recognizing that they cannot gratify them all: some because they are impossible, like being immortal (Aristotle (4) III, 1111b 20–2); and others because the conditions on which one can be gratified exclude gratifying another. Once you have distinguished, however tentatively, between those wishes you can possibly gratify, and those you cannot, according to your present view of the sort of life you wish to lead (a matter of your moral character) you will select some of the former for gratification (Aristotle (4) VI, 1142b 16–20; 1144a 6–9).

The virtuous and the vicious may well have the same wishes (the virtuous hankering for vicious ends, and the vicious for virtuous ones); but their characters are distinguished by the wishes they deliberate about and so probably act upon. They have options, in the sense of having a variety of wishes, of which the virtuous take some for deliberation and the vicious take others. That you take a given wish for deliberation presupposes that you have for the time being opted not to act on the others. Aristotle acknowledged that there will be a further explanation of why you have opted to deliberate how to gratify a given wish (the specific moral character you have developed), but he held that information that you have so opted entitles anybody explaining your choice to disregard your other wishes as irrelevant to it.

The second difficulty arises because Aristotle's description of how questions arise in deliberation has been incompletely understood. You begin by asking: How can a given wish, say, to bisect a given straight line, be gratified? When you reach an answer, you deliberate no further unless a supplementary question occurs to you. Suppose that you recollect Euclid's way of bisecting straight lines. Are there others? Of course, but why should you care? Euclid's will do perfectly well. So you choose it. You will hesitate only if some reason for not choosing it occurs to you; and in most cases none will. That is why formulations of bits of deliberation usually omit both the question whether there are such reasons and the answer that there are not. But strictly they should not. Hence formulations like (A) above are logically defective. Insert the missing question and answer, and the objection will vanish that Watson's wish and deliberation, as stated, do not logically require him to choose as he did.

When supplementary questions do occur, choice is not logically required until they are satisfactorily answered. But it is logically required when they have been, unless the answers lead you to cease to treat your wish as one to be acted on. A number of cases are possible. For example, suppose that two ways of bringing about what you wish occur to you, and you see no reason for preferring one to the other. Well, since you wish to bring about the end, and either way will do, you must make an arbitrary choice between them. Perhaps you flip a coin. Or suppose that you find a way of bringing about what you wish, but that there is an objection to it: it is ugly, or tedious, or immoral, or expensive. Then you must deliberate whether what you wish for can be brought about unobjection-ably, and if you conclude that it cannot, whether you should cease to number it among the wishes you will act on. Or finally, suppose that your wish is competitive: you wish not merely to bring something about, but to do it in a way that cannot be bettered in some respect, then you will not choose any way you find unless you satisfy yourself that it cannot be thus bettered.

It is because of cases like these that the medieval Aristotelians distinguished choice from consent. Aquinas, for example, made a great deal of Aristotle's observation that, in practical reasoning, 'the last [step] in the order of analysis is the first in the order of becoming.' When you reason from what you wish to bring about to some action you can choose that will bring it about, you are reasoning from a wished for effect to a cause that is within your power. But in the causal realm, deduction is from cause to effect, not from effect to cause. Hence the foundation of any piece of successful practical reasoning is a deductive demonstration that the effect wished for can be brought about by a certain sequence of causes, beginning with one that is in the agent's power (cf. Kenny (3), 143–6). And since effects can often be brought about in different ways, deliberation often discloses several different deductions of the wished for effect from causes the agent can bring about. When this happens, Aquinas held that each such deduction yields a practical conclusion to which the agent necessarily 'consents', but not one which he necessarily 'chooses' (Aquinas (1), I–II, 15, 3). Thus he would consider Watson's reasoning in (A) above, as it stands, to provide him with solid grounds for consenting to fry himself some bacon and eggs, but not for choosing to do so.

In the examples of practical reasoning we have been considering, neither premises nor conclusions describe propositional attitudes, but rather express propositions towards which attitudes are taken. But human actions are explained by propositional attitudes, not by their contents. Watson's action is immediately explained by his choice to do it; but his choice itself was the taking of the final propositional attitude in a sequence, and it is explained by his having taken the previous members of that sequence. They were, in order:

B. (1) Watson wished: *that he get himself a good breakfast.*

   (2) He began with the belief: *that fried bacon and eggs make a good breakfast;*

   (3) and, upon investigating, arrived at the further belief: *that what he needed to make such a breakfast was in the larder.*

   (4) He then asked: *whether there was any reason to deliberate further, for example, to inquire whether some other breakfast he could get himself would be better;*

   (5) and answered: *No.*

   (6) So he chose: *that he fry himself some bacon and eggs.*

I have argued that, given Aristotle's concept of a wish that gives rise to deliberation, Watson could not have had the propositional attitudes described by (B1)–(B5) and consistently have believed it to be reasonable to refuse to take that described by (B6). (Of course, the derivation is not formal: for example, it is not explicitly stated that Watson believed that he could make use of what is in the larder. But it would be frivolous to demand formalizations as boring as they are ready to hand.) Yet even if that is so, and even if Watson had all six attitudes in the appropriate sequence, it would not follow that the sixth would be correctly explained by the first five. As Aristotle insisted, it is possible to go through a piece of practical reasoning that logically requires a certain choice, and yet not make that choice. Under what conditions does a sequence of propositional attitudes that would make a choice reasonable also explain it? This question will be answered in chapter 7; but much must be done before it can be given.

The first thing that must be done is to observe a deficiency in such explanations as (B) above, and correct it. Both observation and correction were first made by the medieval Aristotelians. As set out in (B), Watson takes only two orectic attitudes, and they are discontinuous. He begins by taking one: he wishes for an end. Next, he engages in a non-orectic process of deliberation, in which he forms or calls to mind a number of beliefs, and by means of them, reaches a belief about how that end can be brought about. As a result, he takes a second orectic attitude: he chooses to do what, according to the belief he has reached, will bring it about. But is the process between originating wish and concluding choice entirely non-orectic? The medieval Aristotelians could not believe it. Taking the option of deliberating about one wish and not others is itself orectic: it changes 'Wouldn't that be nice!' to 'I can and will bring it about, but how?' Do none of the later stages of deliberation have orectic accompaniments as well?

The classical medieval treatment of this question is Thomas Aquinas's. You cannot deliberate about an end you believe to be attainable without taking an orectic attitude towards it that is distinct from wishing for it: the attitude of 'willing' to bring it about in whatever way your deliberation shows you. Ruminations about bringing it about are not deliberations how *to* do it unless they are processes of planning in the light of which you look forward to acting. Aquinas followed his twelfth century predecessors in using the word 'intention' for the attitude of willing to bring about a wished for end in whatever way deliberation may conclude. You may intend an end without having much idea of how to attain it, but you cannot continue to intend it unless you continue to deliberate until you reach a conclusion about how to attain it. The line between idle wishes and intentions about which you deliberate only fitfully is hard to draw; but it is clear that a mark of intending an end is that your planning is practical, and that you are committed to carrying out its result (Aquinas (1), I–II, 12, 1–4).

Deliberation is therefore the process of planning that develops an intention from something indeterminate to a choice that can be acted on. As J.L. Austin pointed out, that the idea of something like planning is inseparable from that of intending is shown by the different ways in which we speak of purposes and intentions: purposes are realized or not; intentions, like plans, are carried out or not (Austin, 283–5). In the course of deliberating, you may find several more or less determinate ways by which you can attain your end that you would accept if there were nothing better: ways you 'consent to', while deferring choice until you have answered the supplementary practical questions they raise: for example, whether there is an easier or less costly way of attaining it. These questions must be limited: if you continue indefinitely to find new questions, your intention, if you ever really had it, will lapse. When you have answered them, you have formed a definite plan; and if, when you see what that plan entails, you persist in wishing to bring about your original end, your intention has become fully determinate. Such an intention is identical with what Aristotle called a choice (Aquinas (1), I–II, 12, 4).

In Aquinas's treatment, to intend is always to intend an end by way of something that is for the sake of that end. In creating what was to become the everyday concept of intending, he and the other medieval Aristotelians had no colloquial usage to guide them. They thought of themselves as completing a theory of Aristotle's. By contrast, most philosophers in our century have begun by examining how the verb 'to intend' and its cognate noun, adjective and adverb are colloquially used.

Anscombe led the way by picking out three forms of speech as crucial. Here are examples of them.

(1) When Socrates said that he was going to remain in prison and accept his sentence, he was expressing an intention.
(2) Socrates remained in prison and accepted his sentence with the intention of doing what was best for Athens.
(3) Socrates' remaining in prison was intentional.

'It is implausible,' she correctly observed, 'to say that the word is equivocal as it occurs in these different cases' (Anscombe (1), 1). But, if they are not equivocal, which most illuminates the concept all express?

Anscombe herself, choosing the often profitable strategy of

working as far as possible with cases in which what is talked about is observable, spent most of her time with (2), using her conclusions in investigating (3). Although she began with expressions of intention such as are described in (1), she wrote little about what they express. Those who took example by her for the most part concluded that there are no such things as intentions. They acknowledged that by speaking of intentions certain sorts of explanation of behaviour can be expressed, namely, those to which Socrates draws attention in the *Phaedo*. But they insisted that this no more shows that there are such entities as intentions than that we can express certain statistical truths about human beings as a set by speaking of the average human being shows that there is such an entity as the average human being. In neither case do our apparently referential expressions stand for anything.

Following this line of thought, Alan White wrote of verbs such as 'wonder', 'hope' and 'expect', of which 'intend' is one, that it is important to show

> first, that these verbs are not the names of specific and mysterious internal operations but polymorphous descriptions of an indeterminate set of unmysterious and publicly observable actions; and, secondly, that to be conscious of these operations is not to spectate them, but to be knowingly and actively engaged in them and, therefore, in the various public acts in which they are manifested (White, 74).

But there are fatal objections to treating 'intend' in this way.

One of them, which depends on what explaining an action is, must be deferred until chapter 7. But another, decisive in itself, has been pointed out by Davidson: namely, that there is such a thing as pure intending, 'intending without conscious deliberation or overt consequence.' At noon, on the spur of the moment, you form the intention of going to the swimming pool between five and six o'clock, and at two a friend calls and you abandon your intention. You could truly say, 'That afternoon,

I intended until you called to go to the pool between five and six.' And yet no action came of your intention. Once such cases are recognized, 'there is no reason not to allow that intention of exactly the same kind is also present when the intended action eventuates' (Davidson (1), 89).

Why have so few philosophers in the analytic tradition drawn the obvious inference from such cases? The passage I have quoted from White, which is representative, suggests an answer. They have assumed that any 'operation' that is neither publicly observable nor immediately felt (like sensations of pressure, heat and cold, and the like) is mysterious; and that such mysterious processes can intelligibly be supposed to be known only by some sort of inner sense, which there is good reason to deny that we possess.

That our knowledge of our intellectual life is not by inner sense is plain enough. What calls for criticism is the concept of public observability. In any natural language, as Anscombe has pointed out, many of the verbs by which happenings in the physical world are described are causal (consider 'crush', 'bend', 'burn', 'fetch'). All these are used to describe happenings that are publicly observable, yet applying any of them to a given event, for example, 'fetching' to Jack's bringing a pail of water from the well up the hill, can be justified only by assuming much that cannot be ascertained by observing that happening (cf. Anscombe (2), II, 137). What are commonly called 'publicly observable' happenings would more perspicuously be described as happenings that can confidently be reported as observed provided that a number of defensible assumptions are made about the nature of the things observed and the state of the observers. But those assumptions can only be defended holistically, as part of a body of beliefs that together make more sense of what we observe than any alternative body known to us. This, incidentally, is a further implication of Quine's and Davidson's theme that the truth of almost any sentence presupposes the truth of numerous others.

What is true of inanimate physical objects is also true of animals, both rational and non-rational. The verbs in all civilized languages in which their behaviour is described are explanatory. That an animal desires, likes, dislikes, fears, hates, hopes and tries to do or to avoid are often publicly observable, provided that a number of defensible assumptions about their nature are made. What is extraordinary about the assertion that these verbs are merely 'polymorphous descriptions of . . . publicly observable actions' is its neglect of their rich explanatory content. The theory of that content may not be traceable to known theorists (although the introduction of the concept of intending is an exception). It is 'folk' theory. But folk theory is not confined to the surface of things.

Examination of the texts of Plato, Aristotle and the medieval Aristotelians shows that what they wrote about human action is consistent with these non-empiricist commonplaces. Aquinas is the best example of the three, because he employs more concepts in explaining human action than the other two. Yet he explains none of those concepts by giving directions for introspecting specimen mental events to which it applies, or by referring to anybody's introspective reports. Instead, he reminds us of what is commonly believed about the ways in which human actions can fail or come off. It is commonly believed that a human being can wish to attain an end, and yet not bother to consider means at all; that he can think about suitable ways to attain it and yet not settle on any as suitable; that he can decide that some way of attaining it is most suitable and yet not choose to take it; and, finally, that he can choose to take the way of attaining his end he judges most suitable, and yet find that he has misjudged it, whether from ignorance of the world or of his own powers.

A false and deeply confused doctrine that was philosophically fashionable is still encountered: namely, that taking propositional attitudes and persisting in them are items in one's flow of private consciousness, which are named by private ostensive definition, and which have complex causal relations with one's bodily states. But although that doctrine is false (the Wittgensteinian reasons why it is are familiar, and need not be repeated), it does not follow that descriptions of actions in terms of their doers' propositional attitudes can be analysed without residue in terms of patterns of their surface behaviour.

Why do we believe that human beings have wishes, beliefs and intentions at all? Not because, having introspected and privately named them, we somehow discover that we all introspect the same things and replace our private names with public ones. And not because striking features of observable behaviour can only be explained by invoking them. Such explanations put the cart before the horse. Rather, it is because human beings in all cultures, certainly in all civilized ones, are brought up to understand one another's behaviour as not carrying its explanation on its face, but as arising from complex sets of propositional attitudes. Not all cultures, it is true, have developed philosophical theories of action. But I know of no civilized culture in which people do not interpret one another's behaviour in part in terms of concepts that either coincide with, or are specific forms of, those of wishing for ends, believing that something is the case, and intending to bring about something wished for in accordance with some plan.

Learning to interpret one another's behaviour in this way goes with learning how, without studying our own behaviour, both to identify our own propositional attitudes, and to express them to others. In discussing what he calls 'avowals' Ryle recognized this.

> [I]n its primary employment 'I want . . .' is not used to convey information, but to make a request or demand . . . Nor, in their primary employment are 'I hate . . .' and 'I intend . . .' used for the purpose of telling the hearer facts about the speaker; or else we should not be surprised to hear them uttered in the cool,

informative tones of voice in which we say 'he hates . . .' and
'they intend'. . . . They are things said in detestation and
resolution and not things said in order to advance biographical
knowledge about detestations and resolutions (Ryle, 183–4).

Human beings could not have developed the elaborate
systems of interpreting one another's behaviour in terms of
propositional attitudes if they were not able to 'avow' those
attitudes when they have them. And Ryle properly points out
that the primary employment of such avowals is expressive,
and not informative. But it does not follow that your avowals
of wishes or intentions are merely behavioural indications of
those attitudes. As Ryle elsewhere wrote of avowals of moods,
they are 'not merely one fairly reliable index among others',
but 'the first and best index' (Ryle, 103). Behavioural indications can be variously interpreted; but, in normal cases,
avowals of propositional attitudes are either reliable or they
are lies.

It is no more open to us to cease to avow our propositional
attitudes, to treat the avowals of others as normally either
reliable or deceitful, and to interpret the actions of others as
arising from their propositional attitudes, as evidenced by
their avowals, their other behaviour, and their past lives, than
it is open to us to cease to believe that the earth existed for
many years before we were born. We may, it is true, improve
upon all these practices, as our culture has improved upon the
ways in which its predecessors explained various physical
phenomena. But nobody, as far as I know, has explained how
human beings could live anything like human lives without
interpreting one another's behaviour as arising from propositional attitudes. As Wittgenstein remarked:

> Giving grounds . . . comes to an end; – but the end is not
> certain propositions striking us immediately as true, i.e. it is not
> a kind of *seeing* on our part; it is our *acting* which lies at the
> bottom of the language-game (Wittgenstein (3), #209).

That is why our way of interpreting one another's behaviour is immune to scepticism.

CHAPTER 4

PROPOSITIONAL ATTITUDES: FREGE'S SEMANTICS REVISED

It is by deliberating how to bring about ends they wish for that human beings make the choices, or determinate intentions, by which their actions are explained. Yet, while the truth of at least some of their beliefs, and the validity of at least some of their inferences from them, presumably make some difference to their choices, the propositions about which they deliberate are true or false independently of their believing them, and the inferences they draw are valid or invalid independently of their drawing them. Explanations of action in the Socratic tradition seem therefore to belong to two worlds: the world of propositions and their logical relations, and the world of everyday events in which human beings take attitudes. Are such hybrids intelligible? And if they are, how do they explain everyday events like actions?

These questions cannot be answered, as they will be in chapter 7, until two others are. First, how is choosing to do something related to doing it? And secondly, how are the beliefs arrived at by deliberation related to the increasingly determinate intentions they generate? These further questions cannot be answered until the semantical foundation for doing so has been laid: until it has been established what is being said when a propositional attitude is ascribed to somebody. In the jargon of semantics: what are the truth-conditions of ascriptions of propositional attitudes?

For reasons already given, the semantical theory with which I shall work is Fregean. The particular form of it is largely Michael Dummett's, although I shall also draw upon Leonard Linsky's illuminating examination of Frege's theory of intentional contexts in relation to Russell's. A number of alternatives to Fregean semantics have been proposed. Yet Dummett's and Linsky's investigations show how robust it is. Much that has been thought fatal to it, far from being so, throws new light on how it should be interpreted. An example we have already had reason to consider is Quine's demonstration of the indeterminacy of translation.

Frege's point of departure was what the essential function of any language is to enable its speakers to make utterances that are true or false. Nothing that does not so equip them is a language, no matter what else it enables them to do; and anything that does is a language, no matter what else it fails to enable them to do. All true or false utterances are of sentences, and hence are complex. For all sentences are made up of parts having different semantic roles – that is, which contribute in different ways to the truth-value (the truth or falsity) of the uttered sentence. The most primitive sentences, those out of which all others are constructed, are composed of expressions having one or the other of two kinds of role: either that of standing for individuals (as do names or what Russell called definite descriptions), or that of being true or false of individuals (as first-level predicates are, whether monadic or polyadic). More complex sentences are constructed out of these simple ones in ways Frege's work was to make familiar: by employing conjunctions and other operators, and by substituting variables for individual names or for predicates and then quantifying.

The semantic roles of sentences and of their semantically functioning parts are analogous. That of a sentence is to be true or false; that of a name or definite description is to stand for an individual of which first-level predicates are true or false; and that of a first-level predicate, to stand for something true or false of this individual or that. How strong the analogy is has been disputed. In his later work, Frege maintained that it is very strong indeed: that the relation individual names have to their bearers is the paradigm of reference, and that sentences and their parts are all related to their referents exactly as individual names are to their bearers. Predicates, he concluded, stand for 'unsaturated' entities resembling mathematical functions; and when the name for such an entity is attached to an individual name, the sentence thus formed also has a referent, namely a truth-value. Accordingly, first-level predicates stand for functions from individuals to one or the other of two special individuals: the truth-values, the True and the False.

A minor amendment is necessary here. Frege's doctrine that the sense of a sentence is made up of the senses of its parts is incompatible with his doctrine that first-level predicates stand for functions from individual objects to truth-values. For senses, whether of sentences or of their parts, are individual objects: routes from signs to their referents. If a sentence can stand for a truth-value only because it contains functional expressions as well as names, the sense by virtue of which it does so cannot consist of the unconnected senses of its parts. But the necessary correction, as Dummett points out, is straightforward. Attaching the predicate 'is F' to the individual name 'a' forms the sentence 'a is F'; and the sense of that whole sentence must consist, not of the unconnected senses of the name 'a' and of the predicate 'is F', but rather of the sense of 'a', and a function associated with the sense of 'is F', which maps it on to that sense (Dummett (1), 294).

Many of Frege's followers find it so absurd to identify the referents of sentences with truth-values conceived as individual objects that, like Dummett, they denounce Frege's doing so as a 'ludicrous deviation' and a 'gratuitous blunder' (Dummett (1), 184). Whether or not we should go so far,

Dummett seems to be clearly right in denying that any such identification was necessary for Frege: that sentences have truth-values for their referents may be taken as merely an analogue of names' having individual objects as their referents, and not a special case of it (Dummett (1), 412). In what follows, I shall not assume that truth-values are individuals. In expounding Frege, I shall occasionally speak of them as 'referents' of sentences, but in doing so I shall follow Dummett, and treat reference as an analogical concept.

Throughout his philosophy of language, Frege was faithful to the principle that the truth-value of a sentence (that is, its referent) is unaffected by replacing any expression in it by another having the same reference (Frege (1), 35–6/163–5; cf. Dummett (1), 271). Since the reference of a name is what pre-Fregean logicians called its 'extension', as opposed to its 'intension', or what determines its reference, this principle is one form of what is now known as 'the principle of extensionality' (cf. Russell (2), 168–9; Quine (1), 151; Linsky, xxi–xxiii, 43). However, the informativeness of some statements of identity, such as 'William of Ockham is the Venerable Inceptor', show either that the principle of extensionality is false, or that sentences do more than refer. And, as Frege was quick to recognize, statements about propositional attitudes have similar implications. Frege gave his own best example of the problem raised by informative statements of identity in an undated letter to P.E.B. Jourdain. He wrote:

> Let us suppose that an explorer travelling in an unexplored country sees a high snow-capped mountain on the northern horizon. By making inquiries among the natives he learns that its name is 'Aphla'. . . . Another explorer sees a snow-capped mountain on the southern horizon, and learns that it is called 'Ateb'. Later comparison shows that both explorers saw the same mountain. Now the content of the proposition 'Ateb is Aphla' is far from being a mere consequence of the principle of identity, but contains a valuable piece of geographical know-

ledge. What is stated in the proposition 'Ateb is Aphla' is certainly not the same thing as the content of the proposition 'Ateb is Ateb' (Frege (3), 80).

The principle of extensionality lays it down that, if 'Aphla' and 'Ateb' are two names of one and the same mountain, then the truth-value of the sentence 'Aphla is Ateb' must be the same as that of the sentence 'Ateb is Ateb'. But, as Frege points out, the 'content' of what they say is not the same. Conveying the same information is more than conveying the same truth-value. Whence springs this difference of content?

The example of the explorers shows us. The report of the first explorer informs you that if you go to the place he reached by the itinerary described in his report, you will, if you look, see on the southern horizon the mountain called 'Aphla'. The report of the second informs you that if you go to the place he reached by his different itinerary, the snow-capped mountain you will see on the northern horizon is the one called 'Ateb'. The important piece of geographical information conveyed by the news that Aphla and Ateb are one and the same is that one and the same snow-capped mountain is visible to the south of a position reached by a certain specified itinerary, and to the north of a position reached by a second and different specified itinerary. What matters for information is not only what the names 'Aphla' and 'Ateb' refer to, but how those who hear or read the sentences containing them determine it. The first explorer explained what 'Aphla' refers to in one way, and the second explained what 'Ateb' refers to in another; and the statement that Aphla and Ateb are identical is informative because it tells us that the referents determined in these two different ways are not different, as might be expected, but one and the same.

Understanding any significant expression in a language, whether a whole sentence or any of its significant parts, is nothing other than understanding how those who have mastered that language determine what its referent is. Given a language in which the names 'Aphla' and 'Ateb' both refer to snow-capped mountains that are the only ones visible on the horizon in specified directions from regions identified in the reports of different explorers, understanding each name is understanding what, according to those reports, you need to do, and what information or experiences you need to acquire, in order to identify each mountain referred to, and how to identify them when you have done and acquired what you need. Frege called what are thus understood the 'senses' of those names (Frege (1), 26–31/158–61). You may understand the sense of an expression and yet not be able to identify its referent. In Frege's example, you may not be able to go to the regions from which Aphla and Ateb are visible; or you may not be able to acquire all the information you need to get there, even though you can specify what it is. It is enough that you understand the instructions for identifying the mountains referred to.

It is tempting but mistaken to identify the sense of an individual name with a description derived from a specification of its sense: to identify the sense of 'Aphla', for example, with a description of the form, 'The snow-capped mountain visible on the southern horizon from a point that is reached in such-and-such a way'. Linsky has pointed out an error in this:

> One succeeds in introducing a new name only if it is being introduced as a *proper name* as opposed, say, to a title, a predicate, or an expression of some other semantic category. . . . It is a feature of the sense of a singular term that it is a proper name. . . . Similarly, an expression's belonging to the category of definite descriptions is a feature of its sense. With respect to these features, any name will differ in sense from any ordinary description (Linsky, 130–1).

Moreover, nothing in the concept of sense as Frege introduced it requires that the referent of a name such as 'Moses' be determined by a single criterion of identification. It may be determined by a cluster of them. If some members of the cluster turned out not to select a unique referent, or the same referent as most of the others, they would be dropped. All that is required is that the referent of a name satisfy either most of the criteria of identification accepted at a given time, or a central core of them (Linsky, 121; cf. Dummett (1), 98–102).

Dummett and Linsky rightly insist that, given the above account of what Frege meant by 'sense', every linguistic expression the referent of which can be determined must also have a sense; for the sense is simply that about an expression by which its referent, which *ex hypothesi* can be determined, is determined (Dummett (1), 293; cf. (2), 478; Linsky, 9–12). This, however, is true only of languages designed for limited purposes, such as the expression of general mathematical and scientific theories. Frege himself, in his later writings, recognized that natural languages contain expressions that make it possible to construct sentences the truth-values of which cannot be determined by their senses alone (Frege (2), 64/357–8). It can be shown that some expressions have different referents in different utterances. However, since an expression has a sense simply as an expression, its sense cannot vary from utterance to utterance. Hence neither the different referents some expressions have in different utterances, nor the referents of the sentences containing them, can be determined by their senses alone. Will amending Frege's original theory to allow for this damage it irreparably?

What a demonstrative like 'this' or 'she' or 'there' refers to in a given uttered sentence is determined partly by its sense; for simply as expressions different demonstratives pick out their referents in different ways. But what referent a demonstrative picks out also depends on various features of the context in which it is uttered: for example, what previous sentences have been uttered, what the utterer is pointing to, and so forth. It is possible, therefore, to think of their senses as functions to their referents from them *and certain features of the contexts in which they are uttered*. And so the truth-value of a sentence, being a function of the referents of its parts, must also be determined by its sense together with features of the context in which it is uttered.

Indexicals like 'here', 'now' and 'I' – expressions the functioning of which in a given uttered sentence depends on the relation of their uttered tokens to the place or time in which they are uttered, or to their utterer – add a further level of complexity. Assuming, as I do, that indexicals refer, their sense is that they refer to whatever has some specific relation to their uttered tokens. Thus it is the sense of 'I' that each of its uttered tokens refers to whoever utters it. As with demonstratives, knowledge of its sense does not suffice to determine the referent of any token of it in a given uttered sentence: it is necessary also to know who uttered it.

Frege therefore concluded that his doctrine that sense and sense alone determines reference must be amended for natural languages. The amendment he proposed in his later writings radically extends a principle underlying his original theory. Since the fundamental working units of language are true or false sentences, the semantic role of any expression that is not a sentence is to contribute to determining the truth-value of any sentence of which it forms a part, he had laid it down that only in the context of a sentence does an expression have reference. This has become known as his 'context principle' (Dummett (1), 192–6). An uttered expression's non-linguistic contexts differ radically from its linguistic contexts. It has a linguistic context as a repeatable 'type'. Sentences, paragraphs, chapters, and the like remain the same no matter how they are repeated; and expressions considered as their parts are similarly repeatable. By contrast, an expression has a non-linguistic context as a non-repeatable individual 'token': an uttered sound or gesture or mark. Yet there are similarities between the ways in which the contexts of sentence types and those of sentence tokens can affect the truth-value of what is said.

A predicate attached to an individual name in a simple sentence stands for a function from the referent of that name to a truth-value. In his late paper '*Der Gedanke*', Frege in effect proposed to treat each token of a demonstrative or indexical expression as standing for a function from certain features of the occasion of its utterance to its individual referent, those features being determined by its sense. In the same paper, he also drew the inevitable conclusion that 'the sense of any sentence containing a part whose reference needs to be determined from the occasion of utterance' cannot be identified with a propositon (Dummett (1), 367; cf. Frege (2), 64–6/358–60). It is economical to generalize this conclusion, and to treat propositions as expressed, not by sentences themselves, but only by their tokens: by uttered sentences. Since different utterances of the same sentence may express different propositions, although they have the same sense, the propositions they express cannot be identified with their senses. They are relativized to the occasion on which the sentences expressing them are uttered.

It follows that, in complex sentences narrating the taking of propositional attitudes such as believing, intending, and hoping, the propositions to which those attitudes are said to be taken cannot be identified with the senses of the subordinate sentences that express them. When Plato writes that Phaedo said that Socrates said, 'I fancy these bones and these sinews of mine would have been in Megara or Boeotia long ago, . . . if I did not think that it was better and nobler to endure any penalty the city may inflict,' the proposition that sentence expresses is determined, among other things, by the fact that the sentence itself occurs in a context purporting to be a report of a narration by Phaedo of an utterance of Socrates. The linguistic context of the twice used 'I' in this sentence, together with its sense, shows that its referent is determined by its being a proxy for tokens of a Greek equivalent purportedly uttered by Socrates. Hence the proposition expressed by the sentence as a whole is determined by relativizing it to an occasion on which its Greek equivalent was uttered by Socrates. It is by grasping the propositions that subordinate sentences like this express, not by grasping their senses, that we determine whether the complex sentences of which they form a part are true or false.

In the paper in which he showed how the concept of sense can explain how statements of identity can be informative, Frege also showed how it can also solve the problems of reference raised by statements of propositional attitude. Consider the following simple example of belief, the most fundamental of all propositional attitudes. In Cicero's *Tusculan Disputations* (V, 16, 47) occurs a sentence already quoted, which may be translated as:

Socrates concluded that the lives of good men are happy.

Embedded in it is a sentence that Aristotle, at least, believed to be falsified by cases like the life of Hector, namely, 'The lives of good men are happy'. Suppose that Aristotle was right, as I think he unquestionably was. If a sentence contributes to the truth of a sentence of which it is a part by way of its referent, as the principle of extensionality lays down; and if its referent is its truth-value, as Frege has maintained; then if the truth-value of what Cicero wrote is a function of the truth-value of the embedded sentence, what he wrote can be true only if the truth-value of the embedded sentence is reversed by what in my translation is prefixed to it, namely, 'Socrates believed that . . .'. But plainly it is not: there are many true propositions which Socrates believed, and which Cicero truly wrote that he believed. Somehow the truth-value of a sentence expressing a proposition towards which attitudes are taken cannot affect the truth-values of sentences about those attitudes. Yet how is that possible without abandoning the principle of extensionality?

The answer is implicit in the conception of beliefs as

propositional attitudes. An uttered complex sentence about a belief says nothing about the truth or falsity of the subordinate sentence expressing what is believed: all it says is that somebody takes a certain attitude to the proposition that sentence expresses. The effect of embedding a sentence in a context such as 'Socrates believed that . . .' is, therefore, not to reverse the truth-value it had before it was so embedded, but to change its referent. Instead of being a truth-value, its referent is changed to the proposition it expresses, by virtue of which, before being so embedded, it had whatever truth-value it had. The principle of extensionality is saved, because the referents of the sentences that appeared to violate it have systematically shifted. Adapting the terminology of the grammatical distinction between *oratio recta* and *oratio obliqua*, Frege described this as a shift from direct to indirect or oblique reference (Frege (1), 28/159; 46–8/173–5).

Both logic and grammar permit additional clauses of the form '*x* believes that . . .' to be prefixed to any sentence that is either true or false. If Frege is right, each such addition changes the referent of the sentence to which it is added from a truth-value to the proposition by virtue of which, before that addition, its referent was a truth-value. Consider the series of sentences formed in this way from any sentence, *p*, that is true or false, with reference to a series of believers *A*, *B*, *C*.

(1) *p*.
(2) *A* believes that: p.
(3) *B* believes that: A *believes that* p.
(4) *C* believes that: B *believes that* A *believes that* p.

And let the numerals in parentheses to the left of each sentence in the series be names of the sentences to the right of them. *Ex hypothesi*, the referent of (1), unembedded in any other sentence, is a truth-value. However, while (1), being embedded in (2), must make some contribution to determining what its referent is, its truth-value plainly makes no difference to it at all. It is true if and only if A believes the proposition expressed by p, no matter what the truth-value of that proposition is. Hence the referent of (1) when embedded in (2) is the proposition which it expresses, and by virtue of which, un-embedded, it has whatever truth-value it has. And so for the referent of (2) as embedded in (3), and of (3) as embedded in (4).

Frege himself held that, with each successive embedding, the sense of the previously embedded sentences changes, so that (1), that is, p, has a different sense in each of (2), (3), and (4). If so, since the propositions they express are partly determined by their senses, presumably they are different also. Hence any true or false sentence potentially has an infinite hierarchy, not only of indirect referents, but also, since all those referents except the first are propositions partly determined by different senses, of indirect senses. Does his theory commit him to this?

Linsky has argued that it does, on the ground that the sense of a sentence, like other things that can have more than one true definite description, may itself be referred to by a variety of expressions having different senses. Suppose that two English sentences, 'p' and 'q', have the same sense, and that their truth-value is independent of their non-linguistic context. Then 'A believes that p' will have the same sense as 'A believes that q', because when 'A believes that' is prefixed to a sentence, it refers to the proposition it expressed before that prefixing. Now suppose that B, although he can refer to the propositions expressed by 'p' and of 'q', does so in a way that leaves him ignorant that they are one and the same. Then B may believe that A believes that p but not that A believes that q. It seems to follow that, when 'A believes that' is prefixed to 'p' and 'q', they do not have the same sense as they have when 'B believes that A believes that' is prefixed to them; for in the former case their senses are identical and in the latter not (cf. Linsky, 54–5). If that is so, then as belief about belief is added to the series without end, at each step new indirect senses of '*p*' and '*q*' appear.

Or do they? It must not be forgotten that the sense of an expression, as Frege explains it, is how those who understand that expression identify its referent. It is not a further expression, such as a description, the sense of which must in its turn be understood.

It cannot be denied that any number of true definite descriptions can be given of the same sense. For example, the definite descriptions 'the sense of the first word in the Latin Nicene Creed' and 'the sense of the word "*credo*" ' both truly refer to the sense of the words 'I believe'. And so it is certainly possible to imagine both that a beginner at Latin may come across the passage in the *Tusculan Disputations* (V, 16, 47) in which a '*Socratica conclusio*' is reported in the words, '*ex quibus bonorum beatam vitam esse concluditur*'; and also that, correctly guessing the senses of the expressions '*Socratica conclusio*' and '*concluditur*', he may work out that Cicero is reporting that Socrates believed whatever proposition is expressed by the words: '*bonorum beatam vitam esse*'. Suppose him, in addition, to dismiss as silly the notion that the lives of the good are happy, and not to believe for a moment either that Socrates believed any such thing, or that Cicero reported that he did. Here, although one and the same proposition is expressed by the words 'that the lives of the good are happy' and '*bonorum beatam vitam esse*', our beginner believes that Socrates believed the proposition expressed by the sentence '*bonorum beatam vitam esse*' but that he did not believe the proposition expressed by the sentence 'the lives of the good are happy'.

Yet this possibility can be explained without postulating additional indirect senses of these sentences. For our beginner, although he successfully refers to the sense of '*bonorum beatam vitam esse*', does not fully grasp that sense. He is in the same position as a reader of the report of one of Frege's explorers would be who could intelligibly speak of the route to Mount

Aphla marked on the map in that report, but who could not use the map because he was ignorant of the conventions according to which it was drawn. Provided that different sentences have definite truth-conditions in the languages they belong to, a speaker cannot fully grasp their senses unless he grasps exactly how to determine whether they are satisfied or not; and to the extent that he grasps with full clarity how to proceed in each case, he must be in a position to compare them step by step and hence to determine whether or not they are the same. If he does so compare them, he will be in no doubt whether or not they are the same.

A final complication. Actual languages, as distinct from Fregean idealizations, contain expressions of which the senses are not sharp. It follows that the question, 'What referent does it have?' will not have a true definite answer for such expressions. And to the extent that sentences lack definite truth-conditions, the question whether or not they have the same sense (express the same proposition) will likewise lack a true definite answer. But that is how, in a good theory, it should be.

Dummett has argued that the semantics of sentences about propositional attitudes can be elucidated within a Fregean theory without resorting to indirect senses. His conclusions, as I understand them, are as follows. For any language, it suffices to postulate one and only one sense for each expression having a semantic value: that is, one and only one route by which (perhaps with regard to the occasion of its utterance) its semantic value as uttered is determined. If those expressions are sentences having certain syntactic forms, then provided that they are not embedded in sentences containing expressions for propositional attitudes, or other expressions having the same effect (there is no need to enumerate them here), their senses determine that their referents are truth-values; and if they are parts of such sentences, their senses determine the contribution each makes to determining the referent of the sentence of which it is a part. Their senses also determine that if they are sentences embedded in sentences containing expressions of propositional attitude, then instead of having the referents they do when not so embedded, their referents become the parts of their senses that determine their referents when not so embedded. Thus there are direct and indirect reference, but only one kind of sense.

Nor, Dummett contends, need there be any hierarchy of indirect referents. In a series of embeddings such as (1) – (4) above, (1) retains the same indirect referent in each of (2), (3), and (4). What A is said to believe is the same as what B is said to believe that A believes, and as what C is said to believe that B believes that A believes (Dummett (1), 267– 9).

Curiously, the commonest objection to Fregean theories of propositional attitudes is utterly unfounded: namely, that it is an *ad hoc* device to save the principle of extensionality, which plainly breaks down in indirect contexts. Perhaps the best-known example is Russell's objection in 'On Denoting', that when Frege introduced indirect referents, contrary to his own theory, he failed to provide senses for them. Russell's point is that it is unintelligible to lay it down that the referents of expression in indirect contexts are their senses in the related direct ones, without showing what is the sense by virtue of which they have those referents. He correctly insisted that, for Frege, there is no backward road from referents to senses, because every object can be the referent of an infinite number of referring expressions. (This sentence is a quotation from Russell (1), 50, modified by altering Russell's renderings of Frege's technical terms to my own: 'denotations' to 'referents', 'meanings' to 'senses', and 'denoting phrases' to 'referring expressions'.) But he did not sufficiently ponder the reasons Frege gave for identifying the indirect referents of sentences with the propositions they express in direct contexts. Not only do those reasons have, in Linsky's words, 'an immediate intuitive and satisfying explanatory power' (Linsky, 45), they also implicitly give the sense Russell complained was wanting.

Far from being *ad hoc*, Frege's theory depends on a twofold observation. On one hand, if Socrates says that the lives of good men are happy, he is saying something true or false about the lives of good men. On the other, if Cicero says that Socrates says that the lives of good men are happy, he is not saying anything at all about the lives of good men, but rather something about what Socrates says. In the two different contexts the same sentence has different semantic roles.

Having made this observation, Frege elaborated the account of sense and reference which he introduced to solve the problem of informative sentences about identity. And, as Dummett and Linsky have also pointed out, he did so by applying his context principle, that only in the context of a sentence does an expression have a referent (Dummett (1), 268; Linsky, 45). If the semantic role of a sentence changes with specific changes of sentential context, that must be part of its total sense. The sense of an expression is not a single road, but a road with marked forks – one fork leading to a view of a certain referent, the other to a view of the first fork itself. The latter fork is marked to be taken if, and only if, the sentence has one of certain specified sentential contexts; the first fork is marked to be taken in all others. Contexts in which an expression is either a sentence subordinated to a principal sentence containing a verb of propositional attitude, or a part of one, are among those for which the latter fork is marked to be taken. Nothing in the concept of sense as Frege introduced it forbids this elaboration. And the systematic connection between the two forks shows that they are parts of the same total sense.

Dummett proposes to revise Frege's theory by laying it down that 'While a word or expression *by itself* has a sense, it does not by itself have a reference at all: only a particular occurrence of a word or expression in a sentence has a reference, and this reference is determined jointly by the sense of the word and the kind of context in which it occurs.'

(Dummett (1), 268). Linksy proposes, as an alternative that 'preserv[es] the basic principle that sense and sense alone determines reference', that 'we recognize for each name just its customary sense, its customary reference, its oblique (indirect) sense, and its indirect reference, which is the same as its customary sense' (Linsky, 67). I discern only verbal differences here: Dummett holds that the one sense, given appropriate contexts, determines whether an expression has its direct or its indirect reference; Linsky that appropriate contexts determine whether an expression has its direct or its indirect sense, and hence its direct or its indirect reference. My wording is Dummett modified by Linsky, but I hope that what I have written agrees with both.

Nor can the context principle be confined to sentential contexts. That the referent of a sentence is an indirect context is determined by its sentential contexts according to its sense shows that it is not determined by its sense alone. And, as we have seen, Frege came to acknowledge that there are sentences the truth or falsity of which is partly determined by the circumstances of their utterance, namely, those that contain demonstratives or token-reflexive expressions.

A further objection to Frege's theory of sense, and one that is widely received, has been made by Davidson. It is that in the formal language Frege offers as a model for natural language a truth-predicate satisfying Tarski's requirements cannot be recursively characterized, because in it 'every referring expression has an infinite number of entities that it may refer to, depending on the context, and there is no rule that gives the reference in more complex contents on the basis of reference in simpler ones' (Davidson (2), 99).

What Davidson here objects to is rather Frege's theory as he stated it, with its infinite hierarchy of indirect referents and indirect senses, than the revision by Dummett which I have adopted, in which expressions have only one indirect referent and no indirect senses at all. Even so, Linsky has persuasively rejoined that in Frege's unrevised theory there is a rule that gives the reference in more complex contexts on the basis of reference in simpler ones (Linsky, 68). And Davidson himself has acknowledged that a Fregean theory revised on Dummett's lines would not assign referring expressions an infinity of referents (Davidson (2), 99). But this acknowledgement prompted him to make a further objection: 'that there is something bogus about the sharpness questions of meaning [i.e. of Fregean sense] must in principle have if meanings are entities' (Davidson (2), 101).

The force of this further objection depends upon how sharp questions about the senses of expressions must be if senses are to be entities. Admittedly Frege himself held that in a properly constructed formal language they must be very sharp indeed. And Quine's work on the indeterminacy of translation has shown that questions about the senses of expressions in natural languages do not have the kind of sharpness Frege demanded. However, Davidson himself has taught us that the indeterminacy of translation does not preclude our arriving at acceptable schemes of radical interpretation. Only if Frege's theory of sense cannot be reinterpreted to allow for the indeterminacy Quine has established, as I have argued that it can, would the fact that senses are not as sharp as Frege thought show that they are not entities.

Davidson, however, not only finds fault with Frege's theory, but offers an alternative of his own that entices by its characteristic simplicity and elegance. When we were in a state of 'pre-Fregean semantic innocence', he declares, it did not occur to us that sentences in indirect contexts could 'mean anything different, or refer to anything else, than is their wont when they come in other environments' (Davidson (2), 108). And so he recommends that we try the hypothesis that the innocent see more deeply than the fallen. Cannot the facts that led Frege to his postlapsarian theory be accommodated by a prelapsarian one?

A syntactic observation suggests a possible way in which it can. Davidson observes that you may intelligibly say,

The lives of good men are happy. Socrates said that.

If you do, you convey something true or false, even though, until you have uttered the second of your sentences, your hearers are left in the air about what you are saying when you utter the first. If you reverse the order, this temporary suspense is avoided:

Socrates said that. The lives of good men are happy.

Davidson's hypothesis is that this sequence of sentences, which anticipates the word-order of an English sentence in *oratio obliqua*, also reveals its semantic structure. Sentences embedded in others containing verbs of propositional attitude are to be understood innocently, as saying just what they do in any context. Socrates, and anybody who truly says what Socrates believes, are samesayers – at least if Socrates ever expressed his belief. And the sentences prefixed to those that are thus embedded should be treated as in parataxis with them, their purpose being to say something about them (Davidson (2), 52–3, 104–8).

Up to a point, Frege could not have objected. Philologists may well conclude that 'that'-clauses syntactically governed by verbs of propositional attitude came into use because the pronoun 'that' was already used in sentences as a proxy for other sentences in parataxis with them (cf. Davidson (2), 106). But he would have objected that such syntactical uses cannot be semantically innocent. Suppose that somebody discussing the history of ethics should utter Davidson's exemplary paratactic sentences:

The lives of good men are happy. Socrates said that.

Should the context make it plain that he does not believe that the first sentence is true, undoubtedly we should take him to be asserting something different by it in this paratactical utterance from what he would have been asserting if he had uttered it by itself.

Davidson maintains that this difference implies no difference in the semantic roles of the sentences he would utter. The two utterances would differ only in the speech acts that would be performed in uttering them – in their 'illocutionary force'. And if the speech act performed in making his paratactical utterance should be true, since he would be saying, in English, the very same thing as Socrates once said in Greek, he and Socrates would be, in that respect, samesayers. Yet he would not be saying the same thing as Socrates did, in the sense of performing the same speech act. Although he would be uttering a sentence with the same sense as one Socrates uttered, and hence one with the same truth-value, he would be *asserting* something different.

Why did Frege insist that the sentences in the two utterances must differ in sense as well as in illocutionary force? Well, what is the sense of Davidson's paratactic sentences

The lives of good men are happy. Socrates said that.

taken together, and without any specification of context? Since the sense of the first would be that it is true if good men as a rule lead happy lives, and false if they do not, and the sense of the second would be that it is true if Socrates said so, and false if he did not, it follows that the sense of the two together would be that they together are true if each by itself is true, and false if either of them is not. Hence if anybody were to utter the whole parataxis out of the blue, it would be perfectly appropriate to remark: 'No, that's false; I agree that Socrates said it, but it's false all the same'.

Frege would have denied neither that somebody uttering the

two sentences together may merely be asserting something about what Socrates said, nor that the context of his utterance may show it. He would, however, have protested that no hearer who so understands what is asserted can be semantically innocent. Such hearers, he would contend, give the first sentence a different sense from the Greek equivalent Socrates uttered: one in which it refers, not to a truth-value, but to the thought Socrates is said to have put into words. That they do not treat it as standing for a truth-value is shown by their not counting its falsity as falsifying the assertion made in uttering the two sentences together.

Davidson objects that this Fregean line of thought is vitiated by ambiguity: the phrase 'what is said' may refer either to the semantic role of what is uttered, or to its illocutionary force – to the speech act that is performed in uttering it. He does not deny that, to the semantically innocent, uttering the two sentences

The lives of good men are happy. Socrates said that.

is uttering a false sentence followed by a true one. But he maintains that this does not preclude the context from showing that, in uttering them, the speaker asserts (truly) no more than that Socrates expressed a certain proposition.

It cannot be denied that false sentences are often uttered without making false assertions. For example, although in uttering the true truth-functional sentence,

If the lives of good men are happy, then Aristotle made at least one philosophical mistake,

you utter the false component sentence,

the lives of good men are happy,

its falsity, far from making your compound sentence false, is part of the reason why it is true. Sentences containing verbs of propositional attitude, however, are not truth-functional.

Davidson must show that true assertions can be made by uttering sequences of simple sentences which contain some that are false. And, in his persuasive treatment of metaphor, he has shown that it is possible, in uttering a simple false sentence, to make a true assertion (Davidson (2), 246–7, 258–9). When your small son has been, not for the first time, eating too much, and you say to him, 'You are a little pig', you utter a sentence which, given that you are his father, he knows to be true only if you are a swine; but he understands that what you are asserting is that his behaviour at meals tends to be pig-like, which has no such implication.

Since Frege's semantics is in principle reconcilable with Davidson's theory of metaphor, why not simplify his theory of propositional attitudes on Davidsonian lines? As I reconstruct his position, Frege would object that the uttered sentences in which metaphorical assertions are made contribute to the truth-value of those assertions by having whatever truth-value they have, just as do those in which literal assertions are made: the difference is that they usually do it by being false, and patently so (cf. Davidson (2), 258). It is because your son recognizes that you cannot be asserting that he is a little pig that he divines what you are asserting by falsely saying that he is. On the other hand, a sentence in subordination to one containing a verb of propositional attitude (whether analysed paratactically or not) contributes to the truth value of what is asserted in uttering the complex sentence of which it is a part, not by having whatever truth-value it has, but simply by having the truth-conditions it has when it is not thus subordinated.

Davidson's hypothesis is that the semantic role of a sentence does not necessarily contribute to what is asserted in uttering it. While his persuasive analysis of metaphorical assertions lends support to this hypothesis, its claim to the title of semantic innocence is disputable. Frege could argue that no semantically innocent theory can so divorce illocutionary force from semantic role; and in his theory they are not so divorced.*

* In earlier drafts I misinterpreted Davidson as holding the demonstrably false position that, although the semantic role of all true-or-false sentences is to stand for a truth-value, it is not part of their sense that they are true. By kindly correcting this misinterpretation, he has shown me that his analysis of sentences about propositional attitudes is robust, but not that Frege's is not also.

CHAPTER 5

CHOOSING AND DOING

In her pioneering study, *Intention*, Anscombe drew attention to a group of problems that are raised by thinking of human actions as doings explained by their doers' choices. All of them spring from the paradox that actions seem to be both chosen and not chosen. Oedipus' killing of Laius, already used to illustrate how the same action can have numerous true definite descriptions, is the classic example. It was both chosen by Oedipus (it is identical with his striking the insolent stranger he met at the crossroads of Phocis, and he chose that), and yet not chosen by him (it is identical with the killing of his father, and he did not choose that). Anscombe resolved the paradox by asserting that an action is intended only 'under a description', which implies, since a choice is the same thing as a determinate intention, that it can be chosen only 'under a description'.

Many were disquieted by this solution, although it is deft and effective. How can something have a property only 'under a description'? How does asserting that some properties are had in this way differ from licensing oneself to contradict oneself about them? These difficulties are removed by analysing ascriptions of propositional attitude in terms of Fregean semantics; for that semantics is independently defensible, and Anscombe's solution is straightforwardly derivable from it.

The paradoxes of choice and intention spring from more

elementary paradoxes of belief. Oedipus' striking of Laius at the crossroads of Phocis can be truly described both as: (i) 'the striking by Oedipus of the insolent stranger he met at the crossroads of Phocis', and (ii) 'the striking by Oedipus of his father'. And two true sentences about Oedipus' beliefs can be constructed which contain these descriptions, namely:

(1) Oedipus believed that: *the striking by Oedipus of the insolent stranger occurred*,

and also that

(2) Oedipus did not believe that: *the striking by Oedipus of his father occurred.*

Within Fregean semantics, explaining this is elementary. The italicized sentences embedded in (1) and (2) do not have the referents they would have if they stood alone (both refer to the True), but indirect ones (the propositions expressed in appropriate contexts by utterances of sentences in *oratio recta* having the same senses). It is irrelevant that both embedded sentences, if they stood alone, would have the same referent (the True), and would contain no definite descriptions that do not also have the same referent (Oedipus' action). In the contexts of (1) and (2), they have different referents (two different propositions), and so do the definite descriptions they contain (their different senses).

Oedipus cannot both have and not have the same belief about the same event. But Fregean semantics show that (1) and (2) together do not imply that he does. He believes a proposition containing one true description of a certain event, and he does not believe a different proposition containing a different true description of it. But there is no paradox in that: human beings can accept some true descriptions of an event without accepting every true description of it.

A useful corollary follows. Complex grammatical predicates of the form, '. . . is believed by *X* to *G*' are not logical predicates at all, and only apparently stand for properties of individual things or events. In fact, they have no referents. The logical articulation of the sentence,

> The striking by Oedipus of the insolent stranger is believed by Oedipus to have occurred,

is not that the event referred to by the definite description,

> The striking by Oedipus of the insolent stranger

has the property referred to by the predicate,

> is believed by Oedipus to have occurred.

Rather, it is that the individual referred to by the name 'Oedipus' has the propositional attitude referred to by the two-place predicate, 'believes that' to the proposition referred to by the subordinate sentence 'the striking by him of the insolent stranger occurred'. The key to Frege's explanation of how the same event can, under one description, have the property of being believed by Oedipus to have been occurred, but not under another, is that 'being believed by Oedipus to have occurred' only appears to stand for a property of an event.

According to Fregean semantics, these results about believing hold for all other propositional attitudes. Hence, taking 'O' and 'A' as any names of individuals, 'F' as any verb of propositional attitude, and 'G' as any complete predicative expression, that an individual O apparently has a property expressed by a phrase of the form 'being Fed by A to G', is nothing more than that A has the attitude F to the proposition that O Gs. Such attitudes are taken to individuals only indirectly, by way of propositions about them. Hence the property of having a propositional attitude taken about it is not a genuine property of anything. This is especially clear in the case of nonexistents. Since it can be falsely believed that there exist individuals satisfying certain descriptions, proposi-

tional attitudes can be taken to nonexistents. Thus Jabber-
wocks can be feared. But they cannot have genuine properties
like being shot: not because they are invulnerable to shot, but
because they are nothing at all. There are no individuals
satisfying the description 'is a Jabberwock'. Yet since it can be
believed that worlds are possible in which there are Jabber-
wocks, propositions ascribing genuine properties to them can
be thought of, and various attitudes can be taken to them.

While genuine properties like being shot are possessed
only by real individuals, properties like being believed to exist
and being feared are merely apparent. Wherever there
is good reason to say, of some property specified by means of
a verb of propositional attitude, that something possesses
it, but only under a certain description, what is thus mis-
leadingly said is simply that somebody has a propositional
attitude of the kind referred to by that verb, and that the proposition to which that attitude is taken can be expressed in
terms of that description.

Since, as Frege remarked, 'it is hard to exhaust all the
possibilities given by language' (Frege (1), 49/176–7), there
are mixed cases. Here is one. The sentence,

> Richard Coeur de Lion did not believe, of Mohammed, that he
> was the prophet of God,

has not merely the sense that Richard Coeur de Lion did not
believe a certain proposition, but also, as indicated by placing
the words 'of Mohammed' outside the subordinate sentence,
that that proposition is about the referent of the name
'Mohammed', however that referent may be referred to, and
that there exists such a referent.

In other cases, the verb of propositional attitude itself has
the sense that the proposition referred to by the sentence
subordinated to it has a certain truth-value, for example, the
verb 'know'. Frege himself discussed a case of that kind,
namely,

Napoleon recognized the danger to his right flank (Frege (1), 47/174).

And there are yet other kinds. They are important for many purposes, but not for ours. What matter for ours are 'the essential reasons why a subordinate clause may not always be replaced by another of equal truth-value without harm to the truth of the whole sentence structure.' Those reasons Frege justly hoped he had 'brought to light' (Frege (1), 49/176).

Just as human beings can believe both that an event described in one way occurred and that an event described in another way did not, even though one and the same event is described in those two ways, so they can choose to bring about an event described in one way, and bring it about, without having the slightest notion that the event they thus bring about has other true descriptions such that, if they knew them, they would not choose to bring it about at all.

Although she spoke of (determinately) intending rather than of choosing, Anscombe drew attention to what this implies when she declared that, in themselves, human actions are neither intended nor not intended, neither intentional nor unintentional, but are one or the other according as they are considered under this description or that (Anscombe (1), 37–43). No more than anything else can an action both have a property and not have it. But, as we have seen, being the object of a propositional attitude is not a property: that an action is the object of a propositional attitude of intending is simply a matter of its satisfying the description of it that occurs in the proposition which its agent intends in intending to do it. It unqualifiedly has every one of the properties it has. That it is intentional under some of them and not intentional under others does not imply that there is a further property which it both has and does not have, but simply that being intentional is not a property at all.

A further consequence is that an action may be intended

under descriptions that it does not satisfy, and hence to which none of its properties correspond. Othello's killing of Desdemona satisfies the description 'the murder of Othello's innocent wife', a description under which he did not intend it; but it does not satisfy the description 'Othello's justifiable vindication of his honour against his adulterous wife', a description under which he did intend it, even though it corresponds to no property of his action whatever.

Davidson, developing Anscombe's line of thought, restated the Aristotelian criterion of human action in semantical terms: 'a person is the agent of an event if and only if there is a description of what he did that makes true a sentence that says he did it intentionally' (Davidson (1), 46). This is plainly compatible with there being other descriptions that make sentences false that say he did it intentionally. Actions therefore form a genuine class, although neither intentional actions nor unintentional actions do:

> [if] a person does as agent whatever he does intentionally under some description, then although the *criterion* of agency is, in the semantic sense, intensional, the *expression* of agency is itself purely extensional. . . . Therefore we can without confusion speak of the class of events that are actions, which we cannot do with intentional actions (Davidson (1), 46–7). [The text of *Essays on Actions and Events* gives 'intentional' for 'intensional' here. I follow the obviously correct reading of the original publication.]

Actions are a class, and every member of that class has both the non-property of being intentional and the non-property of being unintentional.

The paradoxes that arise from treating an attitude's being taken to a proposition as a property of an event referred to by some description in a sentence expressing it are the problems about the relation of choice to action are those on which Fregean semantics bears most directly. But there is another problem about that relation, the solution of which is more controversial, on which it bears indirectly.

A working hypothesis of this investigation is that actions are events explained by their doers' choices, bodily actions being events in their bodies, mental ones events in their minds – whatever their minds may be. But, with characteristic force, John Searle has shown not only that a problem confronts that hypothesis, which, although at first sight merely technical, turns out to be deep, but also that its solution enables us to solve a further problem – the problem of so-called deviant causal chains – which many have believed to be fatal (Searle (1), 81–6, 107–11).

Take an action, such as raising your right arm in voting on a question before a meeting, that you do not do by doing something else. (This is a variant upon a classical example from Wittgenstein (2), I, #621.) What event in your bodily history was it? Presumably, your right arm's going up on that occasion. And what was the choice which, by explaining your arm's going up (a mere event), makes it a raising of your arm (an action)? The natural answer is: the choice to raise your right arm, or, rephrased to exhibit your choice as a propositional attitude, the choice that there occur a raising of your right arm by you. Yet if that answer is correct, it appears to be epistemically circular to analyse your action as something explained by your choice; for 'a raising of your right arm' is a description of an action. If you want to be told what makes a going up of your arm (which may or may not be an action of yours) a raising by you of your arm (which is an action of yours), it is of no possible use to tell you that your choosing to raise it does; for you will now want to know what is the difference between your choosing that your arm go up and your choosing to raise it. Nobody who needs to know what an action is will get much help from the reply, 'The sort of doing that is explained by its doer's choosing to do that action.'

Can this objection be escaped by avoiding the natural

answer to questions about the contents of choices? Let us try. Could your choice in raising your arm have been merely *that a going up of your right arm occur*. No: that would not have been enough. Even though your arm went up because you chose that it do so, its going up might not have been an action at all: for example, it might have gone up because you had asked a colleague to raise it if he saw that you chose to and that your control over it had failed, and he had complied. No proposition that falls short of implicitly describing the event to be brought about as an action will do as the content of your choice; for, given the variety of ways in which one event can cause another, it will always be possible that the event described may be caused by your choice but in such a way as not to be an action.

There is, however, another possibility. If our working hypothesis is correct, then an event to be brought about that was described in terms of it would be an action, and yet would not be circularly described as one. In choosing *that a raising of your right arm by you occur* you would be choosing *that a going up of your right arm occur that will be explained by your choice*. And if our hypothesis is not correct, further probing of the descriptions in the two sentences should show it. True, *you* may not be aware that these two sentences express the same proposition; but, if they do, *we* may avail ourselves of it in analysing your choice. A question, however, remains. Given that your choosing to raise your right arm is the same thing as your choosing that your right arm go up, and be explained by your choice – by which of your choices is it to be explained? Searle has given the only tenable answer: namely, by the choice you are making. You choose that your arm go up and be explained by that very same choosing (Searle (1), 85). Adapting Searle's way of putting things to mine, the choices that explain actions are explanatorily self-referential. This is not epistemically circular, because it does not presuppose that you already know what an action is. It elucidates the propositional contents of your choices to act, which you will ordinarily express in everyday verbs of action such as 'raise', by means of a formula you understand, although you may not know it to be correct.

Even so, as Searle recognizes, this appears not to exclude some of the counter-examples to which its predecessors succumbed (cf. Searle (1), 108). (My treatment of the following counter-example differs from Searle's. He postulates 'intentions-in-action' intermediate between prior intentions (choices) and actions (Searle (1), 95–6).) Plainly, if a colleague,
without being asked, were to lift up your right arm for you, correctly divining that you choose to raise it but cannot, its going up would be no action of yours. Yet it would be explained by your choosing *that a going up of your right arm occur, and that it be explained by that same choosing.* Admittedly, it would be explained by your choice only by way of the intervening action of your colleague: but it appears that an explanation may be self-referential even though it involves an intervening action.

This appearance, which I believe to be superficial, proved unsettling. Some jumped to the conclusion that no theory of action on Aristotle's lines is defensible. Others declared the explanations in the counter-examples deviant, and defined human actions as events in the histories of human beings that are explained by their choices non-deviantly as well as self-referentially. By so doing, they undertook to work out a theory of deviant explanation, an undertaking which Davidson and others have shown to be vain (cf. Davidson (1), 78–80).

As its vanity became evident, doubts arose whether it was needed. Searle pointed out that no explanations are deviant *per se*: there is nothing unacceptable about the explanations in the counter-examples (cf. Searle (1), 139). Why then exclude them by giving them a bad name? Perhaps closer scrutiny will show that, despite appearances, they are not self-referential after all.

Choice is intimately related to belief. With respect to any

choice, there will be certain propositions such that nobody can make that choice unless he believes that they are possibly true: if he believes that they are false, he cannot make it. For brevity, I shall speak of making a choice as 'presupposing' whatever propositions you must believe possibly true if you are to make it.

In general, a choice to bring about a certain kind of event in your bodily or mental life presupposes two such propositions.

The first is that the situation outside yourself is not in the nature of things such that you cannot bring about an event of that kind. If you believe that you are in a well-made straitjacket, you cannot choose to raise your arms. But you can choose to raise them, even though you are in one, provided that you believe that you may not be, and that nothing else may be making it impossible for you to raise them. In that case, of course, what you choose will not occur.

The second proposition presupposed by such a choice is that you control your relevant bodily and mental functions (cf. Frankfurt, 158). This control appears to have two sides. First of all, it is a power over certain of your bodily and mental states, either to persist in them, or to bring about certain changes in them. That power differs in range and degree not only from person to person, but in each person, from one period of life to another. You can touch your toes without bending your knees, and I cannot; but, once upon a time, I could. Perhaps more importantly, many of your choices presuppose that your control over your bodily and mental functions enables you to bring about events in your body and mind that have effects and significances beyond themselves. You can play the viola and solve the problems in elementary trigonometry, and I can do neither; but there was a time when I could solve problems in elementary trigonometry. I cannot choose to play a scale on the viola because I believe that nothing in my power would count as doing so; yet I can choose, probably in vain, to touch my toes or to solve a simple trigonometrical problem, because I believe that there is some chance that I can do so.

Secondly, control over a bodily or mental function is power to exercise that control *or not* according as you choose to exercise it *or not*. If you believe that no choice you can make or refrain from making will bring it about either that your arm goes up or that it does not, you can no more choose to raise it than you can choose that the sun will rise tomorrow.

A choice *self-referentially* explains an action only if it is a choice that the bodily or mental event constituting that action both occur *and be explained by that choice*. In choosing that a certain bodily or mental event occur and be explained by that choice, you are plainly not choosing that it be so explained *even though what is presupposed in your choice is false*. You choose in accordance with the beliefs without which you cannot choose as you do. You cannot choose that your choice should not only explain something, but also explain it because what you must believe possibly true in order to choose as you do is false. Let it be that you make a choice. And let that choice turn out to explain a certain bodily or mental event that would be an action if that explanation were self-referential. If it explains that event only because something is false which you had to believe possibly true in order to choose as you did, then your choice does not explain that event *as you chose that it should be explained*. Hence even though the explanation holds, it is not self-referential.

With this analysis in hand, the apparent counter-examples dissolve. Consider again the officious colleague who, believing both that you choose to raise your arm and that you cannot, takes it upon himself to raise it for you. If both his beliefs are correct, your choice explains your arm's going up, but not self-referentially; for one of its presuppositions is false. Suppose, however, that his second belief is incorrect, and that you can raise your arm. There are several possibilities. At one extreme, he may be so much stronger than you, and so officious, that he grasps your arm in such a way as to deprive you of all control of it. By so doing, he changes the situation into one in which his belief that you cannot raise your arm is correct, and your arm's going up is explained, not by your choice, but by his. At the other extreme, his grip may be so weak that you retain control of your arm, and can move it as you could if he were not touching you. In that case, its going up is explained by your choice, and his officiousness has no effect. Other possibilities range from your retaining the power to stop him from moving your arm, but nevertheless allowing him to raise it, to your choosing that you should both raise it together. None of them calls in question the analysis here offered.

The distinction between choosing to do and choosing to try is also clarified. Whether a drinker recovering from a surgical operation has the power to bend his elbow or not may be unknown both to him and to his physician. To determine whether he has, he is asked to bend it. Not knowing whether he can or not, he exercises the control he believes he may have. If his elbow bends, he has it; if not, not. Yet whether or not he has the control he believes he may have, what he chooses is to exercise it, and not merely to try to exercise it. If it turns out that he has lost it, he is treated so that he may recover it. Treatment results in his once more feeling that he can tense the muscles by which he has learned his elbow is bent. Now he is asked, not to bend his elbow (he believes that he cannot, and so cannot choose to), but to try to bend it: to tense those muscles in the hope that he will bend it. Just so, even though you cannot choose to move a block of reinforced concrete because you are convinced that you cannot move it, you can exert all your strength in trying to move it. If, to his relief, the drinker succeeds in what he tries to do, thus finding that he has regained some of his former control, he can choose once more to bend his elbow, and not merely to try it.

Davidson invented an example that has become a test case for such analyses. This is his own description of it.

> A climber might want to rid himself of the weight and danger of holding another man on a rope, and he might know that by loosening his hold on the rope he would rid himself of the weight and danger. This belief and want might so unnerve him as to cause him to loosen his hold, and yet it might be the case that he never *chose* to loosen his hold, nor did he do it intentionally (Davidson (1), 79).

As described, the example presents no problem at all: the climber was so unnerved by his awareness of his desires that he made no choice at all, and hence did not act.

Suppose, however, that he had proceeded from desiring to loosen the rope to choosing to loosen it, and that, before his choice could take effect, it so horrified him that he lost control and so loosened his hold. Would his loosening his hold not have been explained by his choice? Yes, but not self-referentially. When he loosened it, what his choice presupposed had ceased to be true. He had lost control over whether he loosened it or not. And so his loosening it, although explained by his choice, is not explained in the way he chose.

CHAPTER 6

INTENDING

Until very recently, investigations of the practical reasoning by which inchoate intentions are transformed into choices to act here and now were largely confined to tidying up the work of Aristotle and his medieval followers, and putting it into acceptable semantic form. It had come to be acknowledged, largely because of Anscombe's work, that practical reasoning seldom justifies the conclusion that an action of a certain kind must be done: essentially it is of the form that, given that you have elected to gratify a certain wish, you can gratify it in such and such a way; and that if you do not wish to inquire whether there is a better way, your practical question is answered.

Now, however, largely as a result of work by Michael Bratman, it is also coming to be recognized how complex deliberating about what to do often is. Not only may a plan to gratify a given wish often cover numerous actions over a long period of time, but over such periods a given individual will have several wishes he plans to gratify, and he must decide how to co-ordinate those plans. Not only are good complex plans rarely made on the spur of the moment, for the most part they neither are nor should be worked out in detail. A plan is often put into operation even though its later stages remain to be worked out, and various matters improvised. Not surprisingly, many such plans are either internally incoherent, or poorly co-ordinated with others. The problems of coherence and co-ordination underlie most recent investigations of the formation and revision of intentions.

Objections have been raised to transforming the study of intention largely into a study of planning. Searle, for example, has urged that, while it may do for deliberate intentions, which are prior to the actions intended, there are many perfectly familiar intentional actions for which it will not do at all. Since not all intentional actions are deliberate, not all are planned.

> [M]any of the actions one performs, [he declares] one performs quite spontaneously, without forming, consciously or unconsciously, any prior intention to do those things. For example, suppose I am sitting in a chair reflecting on a philosophical problem, and I suddenly get up and start pacing about the room. My getting up and pacing about are clearly intentional actions, but in order to do them I do not need to form an intention to do them prior to doing them. I don't in any sense have to have a plan to get up and pace about (Searle (1), 84).

That phenomena occur like those Searle describes is unquestionable. But do they compel us to recognize that some intentions are not prior to the actions intended and in no sense involve a plan? The answer depends on two kinds of consideration. First, on clarifying how much prior to the actions intended the analysis of intending we have so far developed requires them to be, and in what sense it implies that they are planned. And secondly, on fuller descriptions of the phenomena.

Austin's statement of the sense in which intending implies planning cannot be bettered.

> As I go through life, doing, as we suppose, one thing after another, I in general always have an idea – some idea, my idea, or picture, or notion, or conception – of what I'm up to, what I'm engaged in, what I'm about, or in general 'what I'm doing'. . . .I must be supposed to have *as it were* a plan, an operation-order or something of the kind on which I'm acting,

which I am seeing to ... carry out.... [O]nly of course
nothing necessarily or, usually, even faintly, so full-blooded as
a plan proper. When we draw attention to this aspect of action,
we use the words connected with intention (Austin, 283).

That the plan embodied in an intention may resemble a plan
proper only 'faintly', and that intentions presuppose no more
than such 'as it were' plans is implied in Aquinas's remark that
'a movement of will that is directed upon an end, inasmuch as
that end is acquired through those things that are for its sake,
is called an intention' (*[m]otus ... voluntatis qui fertur in finem
secundum quod acquiritur per ea quae sunt ad finem, vocatur intentio*')
(Aquinas (1), I–II, 12, 4 *ad* 3). In other words, you have an
intention as long as you have the idea of bringing something
about by bringing about something else. This idea may be as
faint as you please, as long as you have it. And doing
something with the idea that you would just like to do it is the
limit case of such an idea.

If deliberation is what results in anything from as it were a
plan to a plan proper, and if intentions imply no more than as
it were plans then it is far from clear that the behaviour Searle
describes is not planned in the sense implied by deliberation
and intention, so understood. More information is needed
about it. Did the 'I' in Searle's example have some idea, or
notion, or conception of what he was engaged in? Did he feel
tense or depressed as he sat, and did getting up and pacing
about seem to him a sort or release? If so, there was as it were a
plan that he was carrying out. Or was his getting up and
pacing about like wriggling or rubbing your forehead without
being aware of it? If it was, then there was not even a plan as it
were. But was it then intentional?

Robert Audi has gone even further than Searle, maintaining
that behaviour arising from wanting (that is, desiring) or
hoping may be intentional, even though its agent neither forms
nor persists in any intention with regard to it (Audi, 387–8,

400–1). This is plausible if intending presupposes both full-blooded planning, and confidence that one's plan will work. In an unpublished paper, he offers this example. A child whose arm has been injured in an accident, and who doubts whether she can move it, on being asked by her doctor whether she can, although 'she neither intends to try to move her arm nor does anything plausibly called trying to move it, . . . [she] simply moves it in the normal way at the doctor's request.' (I am most grateful to Audi, not only for permission to quote from this paper (a searching criticism of earlier work of mine), but also for discussing it with me.)

If my concept of intending were as strong as Audi's, I would not deny that she intends neither to move her arm nor to try to move it; but I do not think he has brought out all that is implicit in 'simply' moving it. Suppose that, because of the doctor's request, she both wants to move her arm and hopes to move it, but nothing more. The case is hard to imagine, but not impossible. She may superstitiously believe that she has been bewitched, and that something terrible will happen if she does anything but wait to see whether, merely as a result of her desire and her hope, her arm will move. In that case, if her arm does not move, it will not follow that she has lost control of it, but only that she is refraining from exercising whatever control she has. On the other hand, if her arm does move, it will not be because she is exercising her control of it, but because of some other cause; and such a movement would not be an example of her 'simply mov[ing] it in the normal way at the doctor's request.' Moving her arm is therefore something more than its moving as a result of her desiring and hoping that it will move, but what?

The answer implied by what has been said already is that it is moving it as self-referentially explained by her taking an attitude of *orexis dianoetike* to moving it, an attitude that is the same as determinate variety of intending the Aristotelians called choice. Arm movings that are human actions can be distinguished from those that are not as being self-referentially explained by that attitude, although it is weaker than intending in the strong sense favoured by Audi and others. Since what it is called plainly does not matter, there can be no objection to calling it either 'intending' or 'choosing'. But, whatever you call it, it must be recognized as the attitude essential to human action.

Descriptions of ends or means as 'intended', of actions as 'intentional', must have some reference to attitudes describable as 'intentions' in this sense. For this reason, Bratman has happily described intention as 'Janus-faced', with one face turned to the end intended, and the other to what is for the sake of the end – the means (Bratman (1), 404–5). When you opt to bring some end about by bringing about something else, you intend to bring about that end, and you intend to bring about that by which your intended end is to be brought about. And if your intention is effective, you will intentionally do the action you intended to do.

When you do something for its own sake – when the end and what is for the sake of the end are the same – the two faces of intention look at the same thing. Searle's examples of spontaneous action, if they are examples of action at all, could be of this kind. You can get up and pace about, just as you sometimes stretch yourself, because that is what you feel like doing. You have as it were a plan, in that you can say what you are up to; but you are not getting up and pacing about, or stretching yourself for the sake of anything else. Yet these, as we have already noticed, are limit cases. Normally, the end intended, and what is intended for its sake, are not the same.

We all wish for many things which we deliberate how to bring about. And, since deliberation is a rational process, we try to make our various plans consistent with one another. Austin has a memorably amusing example.

> I needed money to play the ponies, so I dipped into the till. Of course, I *intended* (all the time) to put it back as soon as I had

collected my winnings. That was my intention: I took it with
the intention of putting it back (Austin, 275).

This till-dipper plainly intended at least two ends: that for
which he needed money (to play the ponies), and that for
which he planned to put the money back (he does not tell us
what that end was, whether to spare his employer loss, to
escape detection, or something else). He planned to put the
money back in order to make his obscure second end consistent with what he intended to do in order to accomplish the
first. But Bratman has shown that matters can become much
more complicated.

Consider the following conjectural reconstruction of some of
Kasparov's intentions in the decisive final game of his second
match with Karpov for the chess world championship.

(1) After Karpov's fifteenth move, although he only needed a
draw to win the match, Kasparov intended to win, but did not
yet see a way of forcing it.
(2) After Karpov's twenty-ninth move, Kasparov gave Karpov
an opportunity to draw by repetition of moves, with the
intention that Karpov would disdain it in order not to lose the
match, and would weaken his position in avoiding the repetition.
(3) After Karpov's thirty-first move, Kasparov offered to
sacrifice a second pawn, intending, if it was accepted, to take
Karpov's queen's bishop and break up his queenside.
(4) After Karpov's thirty-fifth move, Kasparov played bishop
to queen's rook one, with the intention of forcing a win.

Each successive intention is part of a more determinate plan
than its predecessor. The first of them is an intention to bring
about an end Kasparov believes may be attainable and
consistent with his other ends (among them, not to risk a loss
for the sake of a win), while recognizing that it may prove not
to be both. The second is to give Karpov an opportunity to
frustrate his intention to win, with the intention that Karpov

decline it, and so contribute to the carrying out of that intention. Plans and intentions may include steps that are intended to promote the end, but risk failure. The third is an intention to follow a certain strategy if Karpov replies to his move in a certain way, that is, to do whatever may be the outcome of further deliberation along certain lines. It is not an intention to make any particular move. The fourth is an intention to make a calculated series of moves, depending on Karpov's replies, but in which every possible reply is foreseen and provided for.

All these examples are of intentions not merely to attain ends in the future, but to attain them either by strategies for which the tactics are to be planned in the future, or by moves to be made in the future. There is no branch of human activity, from business to politics to military campaigning, that can be intelligently carried on without planning and the formation of intentions for future actions and strategies. Why is this so? Partly in order to deliberate when we have time to. But, although that is important, Bratman justly insists that something else is even more important: namely, co-ordinating our activities over time (Bratman (2), 25). Kasparov had both a match plan and a game plan. He could not have co-ordinated them unless he had thought out at least his match plan in advance. The more ends we have, and the more complicated are the ways by which we propose to attain them, the more we must co-ordinate them in advance.

As the Fregean analysis of propositional attitudes has taught us, there is no direct road from the logical relations between the propositions to which attitudes are taken to the logical relations between propositions about those attitudes. If it is true that the spoon is to the right of the saucer, and that the knife is to the right of the spoon, then it is true that the knife is to the right of the saucer. But it does not follow, because you believe that the spoon is to the right of the saucer and that the knife is to the right of the spoon, that you believe that the knife is to the right of the saucer. And yet there is a connection. We could not ascribe beliefs to one another unless our beliefs were for the most part consistent and for the most part true. Hence, in explaining one another's conduct by reference to one another's beliefs, other things being equal, we ascribe error and inconsistency to one another as little as possible.

Intention has a place among the appetitive attitudes analogous to that of belief among the cognitive ones. Since wishes do not purport to be consistent with one another, inconsistency is not a constraint on ascribing them. And, since choices to adopt a given means for a given end do not form complexes, choosing to act in one way on some occasions and in a contrary way on others is inconstant rather than inconsistent. You do not contradict yourself if sometimes you choose to deny yourself something in order to benefit a friend, and at others choose not to. By contrast, intentions resemble beliefs rather than choices in often forming complexes. It is therefore safe to infer that complexes of intentions, like complexes of beliefs, can be consistent or inconsistent.

What is it for a complex of intentions or plans to be consistent? It is tempting to look for a property of such complexes that resembles the property in virtue of which complexes of beliefs are consistent. A complex of beliefs is consistent if it is logically possible that each of them is true and that they are all true. But plans are neither true nor false. What property of plans resembles the truth or falsity of beliefs? Their practicability or impracticability. Well, why not say that plans are consistent if it is logically possible both that each of them be carried out, and that they all be carried out? An obvious objection to this is that it is too weak. Plans may be such that it is logically possible that each be carried out, and that they all be carried out, and yet utterly stupid: for example, those that can only work if there is a series of lucky flukes, which the planner does not for a moment believe will occur. And plans for different ends that can all be carried out only by grace of similar lucky accidents are not co-ordinated (cf. Bratman (1), 380).

Analysing consistency in plans as the logical possibility of execution, while too weak in one respect, because it neglects consistency with their planners' beliefs, is too strong in another. As we shall see, co-ordinated plans need not be such that it is logically possible to carry them all out. And it is undesirable to think of intelligence as compatible with inconsistency.

Yet what other way of thinking of the consistency of plans is there? Bratman's observation that intelligent plans must be consistent with their planners' beliefs, while not quite what is wanted, suggests it. The concept of consistency is inseparable from those of truth and falsity, and truth and falsity are properties of sentences expressing propositions. Why not say, then, that a plan is consistent if and only if it presupposes no proposition that is inconsistent? Each plan in a complex that presupposes a logically false proposition will then be inconsistent with itself, and the plans in a complex will be inconsistent with one another if together they presuppose a logically false proposition. But if a complex of plans were such that it is logically impossible that they all be carried out, would it follow that together they presuppose a logically false proposition? No. Let us see why not.

It is because of a difference pointed out by Davidson between the consistency of beliefs with beliefs, and that of plans with beliefs (Davidson (1), 91–2). Bratman was the first to see its crucial implications (cf. Bratman (1), 378–9). It is this. On one hand, you cannot consistently believe a proposition the falsity of which is logically implied by other propositions you believe, even though you believe that possibly those propositions are false. On the other, you can consistently adopt a plan the impracticability of which is logically implied by propositions you believe, as long as you believe that possibly those propositions are false. How can that be? Be-

cause it is not always stupid to adopt a plan you believe to be
desperate: one that you do not believe will work, although you
believe that there is some chance it will. When your options
are either to surrender and be sent to a Nazi concentration
camp, or to attack with at most one chance in five of success,
and certain death if you fail, who can say that it would be
stupid to attack? The implications of this asymmetry reach far,
as Bratman has shown, although I do not agree with all his
conclusions about what they are.

The principal implication, in my opinion, is this. If X
believes both that p and also that q, then he is inconsistent if he
disbelieves their conjunction – that p and q. But if X can
intelligently adopt a plan which he believes to have less than
an even chance of working, then he can intelligently plan to do
a and to do b, and yet not plan to do both a and b. Informally:
whereas consistent beliefs can be validly agglomerated, consistent plans cannot. It is inconsistent to believe two propositions
and yet, when confronted with their conjunction, to withhold
belief from it. It is not necessarily inconsistent to make a plan
by which you intend to do each of two things and yet not
intend to do both of them.

An (imaginary) medieval example modelled on one of
Bratman's well-known contemporary ones shows why this is so
(Bratman (1), 381–3). Richard Coeur de Lion wishes to bring
pressure on his father, King Henry II of England, by capturing, in alliance with the King of France, either a certain castle
in Aquitaine, or a certain one in Normandy. Capturing both
would weaken the kingdom he will inherit more than he
wishes. Unfortunately, he has two forces, of which one can
operate only in Aquitaine, and the other only in Normandy.
The best chance of capturing one of the castles is for each force
simultaneously and at full strength to attack the one in its
territory; but neither has a better chance of success than one in
three. Richard therefore plans that each of his forces attack
simultaneously and at full strength, with the intention of

capturing its objective. But he does so believing that at least one will fail, and intending at most one should succeed. That is, he attacks each of two castles, with the intention of capturing it, because that is his best strategy for carryng out his ultimate intention, which is to capture one or the other; but he does not intend to capture both.

Against this interpretation of his examples, Bratman argues that it would be impossible to co-ordinate plans if we did not demand that it be possible that all of them be carried out (Bratman (1), 385, 398–9). Richard has co-ordinated his plans, so they cannot really be to capture a castle in Aquitaine, to capture another in Normandy, and not to capture both. Rather, we must say that he has only one plan: to capture one castle but not more. This one plan motivates him to attack two castles; but it is not true of either that he plans to take it, although, should both his attacks succeed, it would be true of each that he intentionally captures it. Bratman thus reconciles his examples with dismissing as inconsistent plans the planner believes cannot all be carried out, by distinguishing between a plan (intention) and its motivational potential.

His argument depends on his premise that 'to be well-suited to aid co-ordination, my intentions will need to be, other things equal, strongly consistent [i.e. such that all can be carried out] relative to my beliefs' (Bratman (1), 380). But is this premise true? Why is it not enough that, like Richard, I distinguish between plans that I am confident will work, and others I am not, and in the latter case, sometimes act on several plans which I believe have only a slight chance of success, planning that some, but less than all, will succeed? How does it help to say that the plans (intentions) I believe have only a slight chance of success are not plans (intentions)? Later, Bratman writes that

> There are differences in the role played in [future-directed] plans by an intention to A and that played by other intentions

which include *A* in their motivational potential. Included among these will be differences in the constraints imposed on yet other intentions, given the demand for strong consistency (Bratman (1), 398).

There is unquestionably a difference between, on one hand, intending one of *A* and *B*, but not both, and consequently intending *A* believing the odds of success to be one in three, and also intending *B* at similar odds; and on the other, intending both *A* and *B*, believing both to be in one's power. But why do we need Bratman's concept of strong consistency and his distinction between intentions and their motivational potential to account for such differences?

If agglomeration is not a valid operation upon consistent intentions, as it is upon consistent beliefs, presumably other operations that are valid upon consistent beliefs will also be invalid. It can be left to others to determine which are, and under what special conditions they are valid. (Since they are generally invalid only because adopting a plan implies believing, not that it can be carried out, but only that it possibly can be, there will be special belief-conditions on consistent plans that will permit their elements to be agglomerated.) For our purposes it is enough that the difference between consistent beliefs and consistent plans be appreciated, and that no assumption about the consistency of anybody's intentions be accepted until the whole complex to which they belong has been examined.

From the point of view both of traditional morality, and of common law so far as it has been formed by common morality, the most important question about intention is what features of an action fall within its agent's intention – are *secundum intentionem*, and what lie beyond it – are *praeter intentionem*. In traditional morality an agent's intentions are bounded by his plans for realizing his ends.

Consider the second of the intentions attributed to Kasparov in the reconstruction above. His intention in giving Karpov an opportunity to draw by repetition of moves was that Karpov disdain it, and weaken his position in doing so. Did he intend to give Karpov an opportunity to draw? Certainly, he intended to put him in a situation in which he could only avoid a draw by weakening his position, and in any such situation he could draw. But suppose that Kasparov had miscalculated, and that Karpov had taken the draw: could he correctly be said to have intended to give him that opportunity? Consider a parallel with moral features that are absent from the chess case. A malicious teacher gives a diffident pupil an opportunity to distinguish herself by making a speech on Parents' Day, intending that she make a fool of herself. When she does distinguish herself, can he truthfully claim to have intended to give her an opportunity to do so? The traditional answer is that he cannot.

These examples, I contend, show that what is intended in an action depends on what the agent plans, and not on what he recognizes may happen if his plan miscarries. It does not matter whether the plan is evil (like that of the malicious teacher), or good (as Kasparov's was from a chess-lover's point of view – morally, it was neutral). In neither case does the agent intend to bring about a situation that can develop *either* as a planned *or* not: his intention is to create one that will develop as planned. Each could have done exactly what he did, but with a different intention. That is why what each intentionally did is not a matter of what they did, but of how what they did is described in the propositions they intended.

Foreseen side-effects of intended actions provide another range of examples. As Bratman points out, if you intend to run a marathon and believe that you will thereby wear down your sneakers, it does not in the least follow that you intend to wear down your sneakers. That is no part of your plan (Bratman (1), 399–400). However, consistently with his conclusion that you intentionally do whatever what you intend has the potential to motivate, even though you do not intend it, he is inclined to say that whatever you are vividly aware of doing, you do intentionally.

> Perhaps this is clearest [he observes] in a case with two further features. First, I not only believe I will wear them down; I consciously note this while I am running. Second, wearing them down has some independent significance to me; perhaps they are a family heirloom. In a case with these two further features, I think we would classify my action as intentional (Bratman (1), 400).

He fully acknowledges that cases with these two features need not be cases of intending. Your wearing down your sneakers is not part of your plan – of what you are up to. I see no good reason for regarding them as intentional either. If your sneakers were your grandfather's, and precious to you on that account, and if you are wearing them only because they are the only ones you have, and would not be running the wretched marathon at all unless you promised him to, far from intentionally wearing them down, you may hope against hope that the wear and tear on them is less than you believe.

In a celebrated paper in which he recommended allowing the language we use for practical purposes in everyday life to have the first word on philosophical questions, Austin made much of the reported remarks of the prisoner, counsel and judge in the case *Regina* v. *Finney*. Of counsel and judge he remarked that both 'make very free use of a large number of terms of excuse, using several as though they were, and even stating them to be, indifferent or equivalent when they are not, and presenting as alternatives those that are not,' adding that 'the learned judge's concluding direction is a paradigm of these faults.' Finney, the prisoner, he praised as 'an evident master of the Queen's English', who was 'explicit as to each of his acts and states, mental and physical', and who 'use[d] different, and the correct, adverbs in connexion with each'

(Austin, 197, cf. 185). The moral is daunting. Philosophers who rely on what they are now not ashamed to call their 'intuitions' about the appropriateness or inappropriateness of a word to a given context more often resemble judge and counsel than they do the prisoner. The first word that ordinary language should indeed be allowed to have is hard to pick out from the learned flood of muddle and inaccuracy. In trying to distinguish what uses of 'intend' and its cognates are accurate, a little philosophy may be a better guide than what we spontaneously say when presented with examples.

So far no distinction has been drawn between the kind of attitude exemplified by intending in the future to bring about some end by some means, and that exemplified by intending here and now to do so. There is a difference between the two, of course, but it has been presumed to be a difference between their propositional contents, and not between the attitudes as such. Searle has rejected this presumption. Although he fully acknowledges the importance of intentions prior to action, Searle contends that there is another sort of intention which he calls 'intention in action' (Searle (1), 84).

His first reason for drawing this distinction is that although prior intentions are necessarily arrived at by deliberation, utterly unplanned spontaneous actions are intentional, and the intentions that make them so cannot be prior to them. I have already argued, following Austin, that the 'plan' with which somebody does something need to be no more than what he thinks of himself as doing, whether or not he expresses it even to himself: it need not be at all 'full-blooded'. And, as O'Shaughnessy has remarked, intentions could only be directed towards acts located wholly in the present if those acts were wholly extensionless. Intentions directed towards actions in progress are towards that sector of them that remains in the future. A man swimming the Channel who has got half way across cannot any longer intend to swim the first half: he intends to swim the Channel, but by swimming the rest of the way (O'Shaughnessy, II, 312–12).

The question of the priority of intentions is, however, secondary. It does not matter whether or not the intentions with which spontaneous actions are performed are noticeably prior to them. Actions follow very rapidly upon intentions to act at once, and spontaneous intentions to act are rapidly formed. What matters is whether they differ in kind, and not merely in propositional content, from those that are noticeably prior. Searle's second reason addresses this question:

> even in cases where I have a prior intention to do some action there will normally be a whole lot of subsidiary actions which are not represented in the prior intention but which are none the less performed intentionally. For example, suppose I have a prior intention to drive to my office, and suppose as I am carrying out this prior intention I shift from second gear to third gear. Now I formed no prior intention to shift from second to third. When I formed my intention to drive to the office I never gave it a thought. Yet my action of shifting gears was intentional . . . I had an intention in action to shift gears, but no prior intention to do so (Searle (1), 84–5).

The example is instructive, because it draws attention to the fact that deliberation about how to bring about an end can reach a point at which it gives rise to a choice to perform the first of a series of actions for the sake of that end, even though what more is to be done awaits further deliberation. Your wish to drive to your office gives rise to an intention to drive there by going to the garage for your car, and following your customary route. That intention cannot provide for most of the various choices you will have to make as you drive, because you cannot foresee what they will be, although you can plan a strategy: to get there as fast as (legally?) possible, or with as little fuss as possible, or something else. Suppose that you do not make up your mind about your strategy until you see what the traffic is like, would not your decision count as a prior intention in the later part of your drive? And when, driving in the right lane to avoid being held up by cars waiting to make left turns, you see a bus ahead about to stop, and decide to change lanes, do you not form an intention prior to changing lanes, even though you had no idea of doing so when you went to the garage?

Searle's example is instructive in a second way. Having got rid of the absurd idea that no intention to perform an action in a series initiated by an originating prior intention can occur before that action unless it is included in the originating intention, what of actions in that series of which you are barely aware at all? An experienced driver does not think of the gear shifts he makes as he gets under way. On the other hand, a beginner does.

Does it follow that, according to Aristotelian theories of action, beginners act in shifting gears as they get under way, but that experienced drivers do not? Not at all. Remember that actions are events self-referentially explained by choices, according to what is presupposed in those choices about the agent's situation, control over his bodily and mental operations, and abilities. An experienced driver is one who has the ability to shift gears without thinking about how to do it, and who believes that he has. In shifting gears, he will of course smoothly co-ordinate the movements of his hand on the stick with those of his foot on the clutch, but he will not think about how he does so: he can do that without thinking about how. Does he intentionally co-ordinate his hand and foot movements? Not under that description. When he gets under way, he does not even intentionally move from second gear through third to top under that description: he simply moves into top.

There is no action that does not have true descriptions under which its agent has no intention to perform it. It should therefore be no surprise that descriptions of any action can be found under which its agent has no immediately prior intention to perform it. A good recipe for finding such descriptions is to describe the action in terms that are less functional than those in which the agent's ability with respect to them is described. Thus, if the agent can shift from first to second, describe what he does, not as shifting of gears, but as a movement of the stick in such and such a direction. But finding such descriptions cannot show that the making of the movements described is not intended under some other description. Searle has given no reason to suppose that any gear shift he makes on going to the office is not according to '*as it were* a plan, an operation-order or something of the kind on which [he's] acting, which [he is] seeking to put into effect, carry out in action' (Searle, 283). And if that is so, then there is no difference in kind between his intention in doing so and a prior intention to do so.

There is a fundamental reason for resisting any theory according to which the intentions that are implicit in plans, and hence are often discernibly formed before those plans are carried out, are different from what is intended in the actions by which those plans are carried out; and I cannot improve upon Davidson's statement of it.

> [C]onsider some simple action, like writing the word 'action'. Some temporal segments of this action are themselves actions: for example, first I write the letter 'a'. This I do with the intention of initiating an action that will not be complete until I have written the rest of the word. It is hard to see how the attitude towards the complete act which I have as I write the letter 'a' differs from the pure intention I may have had a moment before. To be sure, my intention has now begun to be realized, but why should that necessarily change my attitude? (Davidson (1), 88).

When Davidson wrote that, he did not repudiate his earlier opinions that 'we perform many intentional actions without forming an intention to perform them, and [that] often intentional action is not preceded by an intention' (*ibid.*).

Waiving the question whether intentions must precede the actions they explain, once the notion is discarded that the plan underlying an intention must be full-blooded, there is no reason at all to believe either that there can be intentional action without intentions, or that intentions can come to be without being formed.

CHAPTER 7

RATIONALIZING AND EXPLAINING

So far, I have avoided the question how (sometimes at least) choosing to do something explains doing it, even though it is fundamental. It is easy for philosophers to find themselves at cross-purposes about it. If they disagree about the category to which doings (and other events) belong, some conceiving them as facts, or as like facts, and others as individual objects, then, when they utter the sentence, 'What sort of doing is an action?' they will not ask the same question. And even when they stipulate that the doings and other happenings they speak of are individuals admitting of a variety of true definite descriptions, so that they are asking the same question, those that answer it by uttering the sentence, 'The sort that is explained by its doer's choosing to do it', may not all be giving the same answer. Some may be answering, 'The sort for which what the doer chose (namely, that he bring about the end E by doing A as self-referentially explained by his choosing) contains a good reason for his doing it (that it is of the kind A, and a doing of the kind A will bring about the end E)'. Others may be answering, 'The sort for which its doer's choice is the self-referential cause.'

This ambiguity, it has already been remarked, may be found in the passage in the *Phaedo* from which the theory of action springs. Is Socrates there explaining his remaining in prison by the fact that his end, as specified in his choice, is a good reason for doing so (that not harming Athens is a good reason for an Athenian's doing something, and his remaining in prison is the only way not to harm Athens)? Or is he explaining it by the fact that his choosing to do it for the sake of one of his ends has caused the various changes and persistences in his behaviour that constitute his refusal to escape? Apart from the context of the passage, either answer can be given.

Fortunately, the context settles the question, as has also been remarked, by obliging us to accept the second answer. Despite Socrates' reference to Anaxagoras, which seems to commit him to the first, by acknowledging that, if he had been persuaded that it was not for the best to submit to an unjust sentence, he would have escaped to Megara or Boeotia, 'carried there by an opinion of what was best' (*ibid.* 99A), he shows that the goodness of the reason on which he acted is beside the point. He could as well have acted on a false opinion about the best as on a true one.

When you do something, finding a propositional attitude you take that would give you good reason to do it 'rationalizes' what you do, in the sense of showing that there is a reason for doing it. Here, while appropriating the word 'rationalize' from Davidson, for reasons which will become evident, I depart from the sense he gives it. As I use it, a reason 'rationalizes' an action if it is one on which its agent could have acted. And so I shall say such things as that the different explanations historians give of the same action 'rationalize' it in different ways. As Davidson uses it, a reason 'rationalizes' an action if and only if it really is the agent's reason for doing what he did. And so he can say such things as that at most one of the different reasons proposed why somebody did something can rationalize it. (Cf. Davidson (1), 3.))

Rationalizing what you do, however, does not explain it, much less explain it as propositional attitudes explain human actions – that is, self-referentially. You may have a propositional attitude that rationalizes what you do, and yet do it for some other reason. Or you may have such an attitude, and yet what you do not be self-referentially explained by it. The question is: when does a propositional attitude that rationalizes what you do also explain it self-referentially?

It is not enough that your attitude be reasonable: that is, that it be justified by wishes a person of good character would have, and by valid deliberation about how to bring about what is wished. For your attitude may be justified, and yet you take it for some other reason. Moreover, even though you may take an attitude for a reason that justifies it, what you do may not be self-referentially explained by it, either because it is so explained by some other attitude, or because it is not so explained by any attitude at all – it is not an action. If something you do is to be self-referentially explained by one of your propositional attitudes, it must be because of something over and above the fact that it is rationally justified by that attitude. Because of what?

Socrates' reference to Anaxagoras suggests an answer. Arrangements in a world ordered by Anaxagoras' *Nous* are for the best because *Nous* is of such a nature that it always acts for the best. That they are for the best does not by itself explain those arrangements; it does so only in conjunction with the fact that it is the nature of *Nous* to act for the best. And what does the explanatory work is the nature of *Nous*: if its nature were to act without regard to good or bad, that a certain arrangement was for the best would not explain it. All such arrangements are explained by how *Nous* disposes, and how *Nous* disposes is in turn explained by its nature. Both these explanations are causal. *Nous* causes the world to be arranged for the best just as a fire causes the water in a kettle placed on it long enough to boil: it is its nature to cause the one as it is the fire's nature to cause the other. Until we know about *Nous*' causality, rationalizations such as, 'Perhaps *Nous* arranged this because it is for the best', remain mere conjectures. Only when we know about it are they converted into explanations.

What is causality? Notoriously, philosophers bitterly disagree about it. Anscombe's answer has yet to be improved upon.

> [C]ausality [she writes] consists in the derivativeness of an effect from its causes. This is the core, the common feature, of causality in its various kinds. Effects derive from, arise out of, come of, their causes. For example, everyone will grant that physical parenthood is a causal relation. Here the derivation is material, by fission (Anscombe (2), II, 136).

It seems evident that what you do can only be self-referentially explained by a propositional attitude you take if it derives from, arises out of, comes of, your taking it. But in that case, your taking it must cause what you do. And since most causal explanations are not self-referential, it must cause it under such conditions that the explanation will be self-referential, that is, under the conditions presupposed by the propositional attitude in question: your choice or determinate intention. It is convenient to follow Searle's example, and to describe a cause that satisfies those conditions as a 'self-referential cause'. And so we are led to ask: what must be the case if a propositional attitude taken by a human being is self-referentially to cause something he does? Human beings are not much like Anaxagoras' Intelligence. We know that they are often mistaken about what is for the best; and we suspect that correcting their beliefs does not necessarily correct their appetitive attitudes. But whatever their nature as causes may be, we need to know something about it if we are to advance from merely rationalizing their actions to explaining them.

Despite the weight of these simple considerations, in the twenty years after the Second World War most philosophers influenced by the later work of Wittgenstein, or by the various kinds of philosophical analysis that flourished at Oxford, dismissed the very idea that the reasons explaining a human being's behaviour could be its causes, on the ground that, since neither coming to take a propositional attitude nor persisting in one is an event, it cannot be a cause. It has already been shown, in chapter 3, that the occurrence of pure intending is a fatal objection to this; but Anthony Kenny's contention that neither beliefs nor wants 'have to be an existence separate from the action they explain, in the sense of being separate events in the agent's biography' (Kenny (2), 119) should be noticed. In attempting to justify it, he betrays that he assumes that either mental events are items in what used to be called the flow of experience, such as 'pangs of hunger, pricks of lust or sudden impulses to pluck a flower', or they are nothing at all. About belief, for example, he writes:

> my belief that my wife is in earshot may find expression only in my talking to her: the sentence 'my wife is in earshot' need not form itself in my imagination at any point, nor need I have a more precise belief about exactly where she is. My belief that there is another step may simply be my lurching forward when arriving at the landing: nothing has to be going on in my imagination to make true the statement, 'I thought there was another step'. Like wants beliefs may, but need not, be items of biography distinguishable from what they explain (Kenny (2), 119; cf. 117–21).

And he argues similarly about intending and choosing.

An external objection to this has already been made: that believing something is never the same as imagining sentences expressing it. Both coming to have a belief and persisting in it are exercises of intellect, not of imagination; and nothing in the flow of experience to which either exercise gives rise should be confounded with it. As we have seen, the concepts of propositional attitudes, both appetitive and non-appetitive, are explanatory in function, like the numerous causal concepts by which we explain physical events. And, like many physical causal concepts, they do not describe processes that can be observed except by their vehicles or effects. As Ryle intimated, that we can reliably avow our beliefs and intentions does not show that they are like pangs or tickles (cf. Ryle, 183, 242–3). There is also an internal objection: namely, that patterns of behaviour do not explain the behaviour of which they are patterns. My lurching forward at the landing may be the only observable evidence of my belief that there is another step, but if my belief were no more than a pattern of behaviour of which my lurching is part, how could it explain that lurching, as Kenny acknowledges it does?

A second reason why many philosophers denied that beliefs, wishes and intentions could be causes was almost equally influential. It was that they conceived explaining an event causally as identifying some prior event, and some law of nature, such that the occurrence of an event of the kind to be explained would follow logically from the occurrence of that prior event according to that law (cf. Kenny (2), 115–18; von Wright, 34–8, 93; Stoutland (2), 352–4). The law might be known only sketchily, and hence it might not be possible to exhibit the connection between cause and effect with any strictness; but it was necessary to sketch it. Yet even allowing this, few or none of the explanations historians and social scientists gave of the actions and reactions of those they studied contained the faintest sketch of any putative law. Hence it was easy to infer that, while explanations in the *Naturwissenschaften* are causal, those in the *Geisteswissenschaften* are not.

In his widely-studied 'Actions, Reasons and Causes', Davidson proposed to resolve the dispute by distinguishing explaining events by stating their causes from explaining why those causes are causes. Human beings had a great deal of causal knowledge of the physical world before they knew any laws of nature. Indeed, as he remarked in a later paper, 'Unavoidable mention of causality is a cloak for ignorance; we must appeal to the notion of cause when we lack detailed and accurate laws' (Davidson (1), 80). Historians and social scientists are in that position. They often have good reason to believe that historical agents' beliefs and other propositional attitudes caused them to behave in certain ways, without having any covering laws in mind at all. Historical explanations are causal, not because historians can sketch the covering laws they presuppose, but because they cannot. In a still later paper he went even further, and argued that the laws historical explanations presuppose must belong to one or another of the physical sciences. Hence historians may have no inkling at all of the laws that underlie the causal connections they can trace between historical events, or of the concepts those laws involve, because they are ignorant of the physical sciences that investigate them (cf. Davidson (1), 15–19; 209–15).

Most philosophers who thought of human actions as events explained by propositional attitudes were persuaded by Davidson's argument that such explanations are causal. But not all of them were. G.H. von Wright dissented (von Wright, 93–6, 115–17), and his line of thought has been developed in a valuable series of papers by Frederick Stoutland. Both argue the case with reference to explanations of actions in terms of complexes of intentions and beliefs. But their argument against the causal interpretation of such explanations can be stated in its pure form as an argument that explaining an action of a certain kind by a direct choice (that is, a fully determinate intention) cannot be causal.

Both von Wright and Stoutland accept, for the sake of the argument, Davidson's premise that explaining an event by its cause presupposes that there is a law connecting, under some description, that cause and that effect. Hence if Oedipus' striking of the insolent stranger is explained as caused by Oedipus' choosing to strike him, then there must be a possible description, D_1, of Oedipus' choice, and another, D_2, of Oedipus' action, such that it is a law of nature, perhaps unknown, that every event satisfying D_1 is followed by one satisfying D_2. However, if there is such a law, before we can test whether it is a law of nature we must first know the descriptions of choices of the same kind as Oedipus', and of bits of behaviour of the same kind, in terms of which that law is formulated. And, given that such laws are falsifiable, we can know true descriptions of Oedipus' choice and of the behaviour it explains without knowing that his choice, so described, caused his behaviour, so described. Yet we cannot know what Oedipus' choice was, described as a choice, until after we know what he did that is explained by it. Explanation by propositional attitudes is *ex post actu*. Hence unless we come to believe that we were mistaken about what Oedipus did, we cannot refuse to describe it as explained by his choice to do it (von Wright, 94–5, 115–16). For if we describe him, on the basis of his behaviour, as choosing to strike the insolent stranger, we cannot consistently refuse to describe his behaviour as at least an attempt to strike him.

This argument is introduced by von Wright himself as a version of the so-called 'logical connection argument', which, in its original form, he acknowledges to have been defective (von Wright, 93–4, 195; cf. Stoutland (1), 122–5). At the same time, von Wright implicitly distinguishes his own version of the argument from its defective original.

That original may be condensed to this: since causes must be logically distinct from their effects, a reason cannot cause what it rationalizes, because it is not logically distinct from it. Davidson demolished this argument by pointing out that 'The truth of a causal statement depends on *what* events are described; its status as analytic or synthetic depends on *how* they are described' (Davidson (1), 14). Can this refutation be evaded, as von Wright believes, by reformulating what it refutes in epistemic rather than logical terms?

Prima facie, von Wright argues that the connection between Oedipus' choosing to strike and Oedipus' trying to strike cannot be causal, because the only evidence that you can have that he was choosing to strike is evidence that he was trying to strike. This presupposes that all ascriptions of propositional attitudes are *ex post actu*, a presupposition that has been contested in chapter 3 (cf. also Davidson (1), 89). If it is abandoned, von Wright's argument might be interpreted as reducing to something like the following. One event can be consistently believed to cause another only if it is also believed that there are laws connecting them that are expressible as testable and hence falsifiable hypotheses. Hence reasons cannot be causes, because, since they cannot consistently be believed not to explain what they rationalize, they cannot consistently be believed to explain them by virtue of laws expressible as falsifiable hypotheses.

If it can be reduced to this, von Wright's argument is vulnerable to a variant of Davidson's objection to its original. Let it be true that you cannot consistently believe that what was done with a tool in Hodge's barn caused a cut in that soft branch unless you also believe that there are laws, expressible as falsifiable hypotheses, connecting what was done and the branch's being cut. Can you consistently believe that the hard striking of that soft branch with a newly-sharpened axe does not explain there coming to be a cut in it? Plainly, you cannot. Does it then follow that this explanation of there coming to be a cut in the branch cannot consistently be believed to explain it by virtue of laws expressible as empirically testable hypotheses? Not at all. Of course those laws will not be expressed in terms of hard blows, sharp axe-blades and soft branches, but in those of some applied science. And that was Davidson's point.

Whether an explanation can consistently be denied if you accept the description given in it of the *explanans* and the *explanandum* depends on those descriptions, and not on what they describe. The cause and the effect in any causal explanation that holds by virtue of laws expressible as falsifiable hypotheses can be so described that, if those descriptions are accepted, the explanation cannot consistently be rejected. Hence an explanation of somebody's doing an action of a certain kind by an event described as his choosing to do an action of that kind cannot be shown to be non-causal by the fact that in it the *explanans* and *explanandum* are so described that it cannot consistently be rejected. The natural assumption is that causal concepts are incorporated into the description 'choosing to do an action of that kind', as they are into the descriptions 'hard blow', 'sharpened axe-blade' and 'soft branch'.

And that natural assumption has been anticipated in our inquiry in the preceding chapter into the presuppositions of choosing to do something. Those presuppositions are causal: that the state of things outside your body and mind are not such as to make what you choose impossible in the natural order of things; and that you have such control over your bodily and mental functions, and such ability to exercise that control, that what you choose to do will be done if you choose, and not otherwise. If those presuppositions are true with respect to a given choice, your making that choice must cause the doing of what you choose. Given that its presuppositions are true, a choice to do something cannot but self-referentially cause your doing it.

Stoutland, however, has discerned a further depth in von Wright's argument: it can be read as objecting, not that causal interpretations misrepresent how Socratic explanations are verified, but that they impair their explanatory power (cf. Stoutland (2), 357–67). Davidson acknowledges that, in the laws of nature that connect propositional attitude with the doings they explain, those attitudes are not described as propositional. Laws of nature cannot be formulated in terms of propositional attitudes. Hence, that the same individual event is both a cause of a doing and the taking of a propositional attitude is 'anomalous'. But in that case, Stoutland argues, an agent's having attitudes of a certain kind does not account for the fact that the tokens of those attitudes belong to any causal types and, therefore, given a causal theory, cannot account for the fact that his act is intentional (Stoutland (2), 359).

Or, as he has put it (in a private communication): 'if reasons are causes only in virtue of their physical properties, then there is no connection between their being reasons and their being causes (even if they happen to be both).'

This objection is strong. Since Davidson agrees that between an event's being a taking of a propositional attitude and its being the cause of an action there can be only an external connection – neither a logical one, nor one necessitated by a law of nature – he would presumably insist that a connection that is external, a mere brute fact, is enough. Takings of propositional attitudes, he would maintain, are identifiable events; and we have the kind of non-scientific causal knowledge of their connection with behaviour that, say, cooks had of the causal properties of butter and oil before scientific chemistry provided them with descriptions of them by which those properties could be brought under scientific laws. Against this, Stoutland urges that the cases are not parallel. While the properties by which cooks identify butter and oil are physical, and are lawfully connected with their chemical constitution, according to Davidson himself the properties by which individual takings of propositional attitudes are identified are not physical, and hence are not lawfully connected with the physical properties by virtue of which they cause actions. It is an ultimate 'anomalous' fact that the world is so ordered that, when you reasonably believe that a bit of your behaviour is self-referentially explained by your making a certain choice your making that choice will turn out, for the most part, to be identical with the cerebral event that is the cause of that bit of behaviour. Stoutland is clearly right in denying that either philosophy or science has the right to postulate cosmic accidents of this kind.

However, Stoutland does not object to the thesis that self-referential explanations are causal, when it is considered by itself, but only when it is conjoined with two others: that causal connections presuppose laws of nature, and that all laws of nature are physical. And there are objections to both these theses.

Do causal connections presuppose laws of nature? In her inaugural lecture at Cambridge, Anscombe denied it on the following grounds. Medical science has established that certain diseases are infectious. After you have contracted such a disease, it is reasonable to conclude that it was caused by your being in contact with somebody else who had it, even if you do not know who he was. But not only is there no known law to the effect that anybody resembling you in some relevant respect who comes into contact with such a person will contract his disease, even if there is an unknown one, there is no need to presuppose it (Anscombe (1), II, 133–9). More recently, Searle has argued along similar lines (Searle (1), 132–5).

Learning a natural language, Anscombe maintained, goes together with learning much causal lore; for every such language contains a host of verbs and cognate words expressing causal concepts. Her selection of such verbs in English was: '*scrape, push, wet, carry, eat, burn, knock over, keep off, squash, make* (e.g. noises, paper boats), *hurt*' (Anscombe (1), II, 137). The sense of these verbs, she reminded us, cannot be learned without learning at the same time the sense of numerous substantives standing for kinds of thing that do the kinds of thing the verbs describe; and these senses cannot be learned without learning how to employ these words intelligently in sentences about happenings in the world.

> As surely as we learned to call people by name or to report from seeing it that the cat was on the table, we also learned to report from having observed it that someone drank up the milk or that the dog made a funny noise or that things were cut and broken by whatever we saw cut and break them (*ibid.*).

These observations, which seem to me undeniable, unfortunately make a disastrous error tempting.

If we learn to report causal transactions like drinking or cutting from having observed them, do we not learn what they are simply by seeing them done, or even by doing them? Just how children learn the sense of words like 'drink' and 'cut' is something about which little is known except that they pick it up in the course of doing and observing the things those words describe in the context of others using them, and of correcting their attempts to use them. Acquiring mastery of such words is part of their acquisition of a 'folk' interpretation of the world as a causal system – an interpretation that may be mistaken in various respects, but which will not be abandoned until one that explains more is discovered.

If we interpret the world in terms of the causal concepts embodied in our language, we shall take many of the events we see to be causal transactions. Given that a pair of scissors is a cutting tool, and that paper does not divide in straight lines unless it is cut or torn in a certain way, I take myself to see not merely that this paper is dividing into two neat halves and that Johnny is wielding the scissors as it divides, but that Johnny is cutting the paper with the scissors. I do not consider the possibility that that, without being cut, the paper divides in pre-established harmony with the scissors' closing. Yet if I thought in terms of a principle of pre-established harmony, I would not speak exactly as I now do, even if I continued to use some of my present forms of speech. Anscombe somewhere relates that once, when she said to Wittgenstein something like, 'You have to admit that it looks as though at sunset the earth stays still and the sun moves,' he replied, 'How would it look if the sun stayed still, and the earth rotated?'

Even if, contrary to the above argument, causal connections do presuppose laws of nature, are all laws of nature physical? Unless this is made true by definition, excluding psychology from the natural sciences if it employs any non-physical concepts, I have yet to encounter a good reason for believing it. However, it is beyond the scope of the present investigation to explore the metaphysical status either of propositional attitudes or of the bodily or mental events they cause.

Central state materialists and functionalists will consider takings of propositional attitudes to be material events, and so will perceive no difficulty. Eliminative materialists will deny that there are propositional attitudes or any other mental states, and so will dismiss the present investigation as failing to limn part of the structure of reality. Our practical inability to avoid describing human action in terms of propositional attitudes, they maintain, generates no theoretical difficulty. Anomalous monists, although they deny that mental properties can be analysed in terms of physical ones, agree with central state materialists both that taking propositional attitudes and persisting in them are material events, despite their mental properties, and also that they stand in causal relations solely by virtue of their material properties. I do not perceive how they might meet Stoutland's objection; but it is for them to meet it if they can.

Those who can accept none of the above, like myself, will agree with the anomalous monists that events having properties not reducible to material ones, can, by virtue of these properties, be causally related to events having only material properties; but we shall remain sceptical that they are so related solely by virtue of their physical properties. I do not, of course, know how such causation works. But nor do I know how any of the physical forces accepted for the present as ultimate by physicists works. The notion that philosophers should not accept any power or force as ultimate unless they can explain how it works seems to me a disreputable relic of rationalist natural philosophy.

Choices do not merely rationalize actions, but self-referentially explain them; and they could not explain them unless they caused them. This argument, if sound, cannot be undermined by showing that, if causal connections presuppose laws of nature and all laws of nature are physical, then choices can only explain actions by a sequence of lucky coincidences. What becomes suspect is not the thesis that the choices that self-referentially explain actions cause them, but the subsidiary theses that together with it produce that incredible result. But which of those theses is to be abandoned or modified is not a problem in the theory of action.

There is no difference in principle between seeing Oedipus intentionally (or by choice) strike Laius and seeing a hard blow with an axe cut a soft branch. In both cases what is seen is described in terms of everyday causal concepts (*intentionally striking*, as people do; and *cutting*, as blows with axes do), it being presupposed that the body of causal beliefs implicit in those and related concepts are for the most part true. What I see does not show that those beliefs are true; and, if I did not have them, I should not describe what I see as I do.

Although he has pursued a similar line of thought, for much of which I have followed him, Searle has taken an intriguing turn at which I demur. It is that the causal relation itself is 'experienced' in both action and perception.

Perception, he holds, resembles action in having a mental element that is causally self-referential. Suffering from an hallucination, Macbeth asked himself, 'Is this a dagger that I see before me?' If he had in fact been seeing a dagger, there would have been a dagger before him, and it would have caused him to have the visual experience he was having. The phenomenal character of that experience was internally complex: it presented itself as being caused by something it also presented, namely, a dagger. In Searle's terminology, it presented its own conditions of satisfaction. And it was because its conditions of satisfaction did not obtain that Macbeth's visual experience was not a perception, but an hallucination. He had the visual experience of seeing a dagger, but without seeing one (Searle, 61–2, 95–8).

The parallel with intentional (and hence chosen) action appears to be close. Adapting an example cited by Searle from William James, let the following be supposed. After your right arm has been anaesthetized, your physician asks you to raise it, although unknown to you, it is being held down; you believe that you comply, but in fact your arm does not move. If you were in fact raising it, you would have exactly the intention you now have, and it would cause to happen what you intend to happen. Your intention, like Macbeth's visual experience, is internally complex: an appetitive attitude to your arm's going up as the effect of that attitude itself. As Searle describes it, it too presents its conditions of satisfaction. But because those conditions do not obtain, that intention is not an intention-in-acting, but merely what Searle calls an 'experience of acting' (Searle, 83–90; 95–8).

The differences between the two cases, according to Searle, are in direction of causation, and in what he calls 'direction of fit'. When something is seen, since an object in the world causes the experience of seeing it, the direction of causation is world-to-mind. When something is done, since an experience of action (an intention or choice) causes a bit of behaviour, the direction of causation is mind-to-world. These directions are reversed, however, in the conditions of satisfaction of the two experiences. A visual experience is satisfied if 'fits' its cause: that is, if it represents its cause as it is. The direction of fit is mind-to-world. By contrast, an experience of acting (an intention-in-action) is satisfied if the action it causes fits it: the direction of fit is world-to-mind (Searle, 88–91; 96–7).

Searle freely acknowledges that 'experience of acting', as he uses it, is a term of art. But, since a term is needed, he claims the right to invent one.

> [J]ust as we don't have a name for that which gives us the Intentional content of our visual perception but have to invent a term of art, 'the visual experience', so there is no term for that which gives us the Intentional content of our intentional action,

but have to invent a term of art, 'the experience of acting'
(Searle (1), 88).

He also acknowledges that such terms of art must not be
tendentious.

> [T]he term would mislead if it gave the impression that such
> things were passive experiences or sensations that simply afflict
> one (*ibid.*).

But this word to the wise is not enough to forestall misunder-
standing.

There is no serious objection to calling an hallucination like
Macbeth's a 'visual experience': it was certainly an experience,
and it was visual, as opposed, say, to auditory. It would,
however, be objectionable to call it an 'experience of seeing a
dagger', not because that would give the impression that it was
passive, but because it would give the impression that there
was a seeing of a dagger for it to be an experience of. Calling
that which gives us the Intentional content of our intentional
action an 'experience of acting' is objectionable in just that
way; for Searle insists that, whatever it may be that gives us
that Intentional content, it is not an action, and can exist
without there being an action. And there is a further objection.
It does seem necessary to provide a term of art for what gives
us the Intentional content of our visual perception, since there
is no expression in colloquial use that stands to 'seeing (some
visible object)' as 'intending (to do something)' stands to
'doing (it)'. But 'intention' *is* available as a term standing for
what gives us the Intentional content of our intentional action.
Why invent a term of art at all?

When philosophers find superfluous terms of art more
convenient than colloquial ones already available, all too often
it is because they unobtrusively do philosophical work that
cannot be done under scrutiny. And so it is with Searle's
'experience of action'.

He contends that 'in both perception and action one *perceives* the causal relation' (Searle (1), 126, my emphasis), and that one acquires the concept of causality from this perception.

> The basic notion of causation ... is the notion of making something happen. ... Now the peculiarity of Intentional causation is that we directly experience this relationship in many cases where we make something happen or something else makes something happen to us. When, for example, I raise my arm, part of the content of my experience is that this experience is what makes my arm go up. ... In such causes we directly experience the causal relation. ... I did not *observe* two events, the experience of acting and the movement of the arm, rather part of the Intentional content of the experience of acting was that that very experience was making my arm go up (Searle (1), 123).

Let us rewrite the last two sentences of this, substituting 'intention', or its appropriate cognate, for 'experience' used as either noun or verb, and emphasising passages in which obscurity or error results. It becomes:

> When, for example, I raise my arm, part of the content of my intention-in-action is that this intention is what makes my arm go up. ... In such cases we directly *intend the causal relation* ... I did not observe two events, the intention-in-action and the movement of the arm, rather part of the Intentional content of the intention-in-action was that *that very intention was making my arm go up*.

In Searle's version, 'directly experience the causal relation' suggests that the causal relation is somehow there to be experienced; in the rewritten version, it is unclear what 'directly intend the causal relation' can be, but there is no such suggestion, and that is reason to suspect that Searle's term of art is leading him astray. What is intended is that the causal relation obtain between the intention and the movement – but nobody would choose 'experiencing the causal relation' as a perspicuous description of intending that. And in the last sentence, the continuous 'was making my arm go up' is not a good rendering of the content of his intention, as though intending is like lifting: he intended simply that his arm's going up be made to happen by his intending it.

These infelicities are ominous. But now ask: Does it even seem to follow from the rewritten version that, generally speaking, you directly experience the relationship of causation in intending to raise your arm? Not at all. What is true is that you cannot intend to raise your arm if you have no concept of yourself as cause, and that Macbeth could not have asked himself whether what he saw before him was a dagger unless he also had a concept of how he could be perceptually affected. Whence did you and he acquire those concepts? No exact answer is available. 'In the process of growing up', and 'In the process of learning to speak my mother tongue', are about as well as anybody can do. One answer, however, can reasonably be dismissed: neither you nor he began by having intentions on one hand, and on the other visual experiences phenomenally indistinguishable from seeings of physical objects and then afterwards formed the concept of causality by reflecting on what you had 'perceived' or 'experienced' in having those intentions and visual experiences. In terms of Searle's theory of Intentionality, the concept of causality belongs to the 'network' of concepts and propositions to which your and his propositional attitudes are internally related (cf. Searle (1), 65–71).

Choosing often self-referentially causes action, but not always, because choices are not always, but often, made with causal presuppositions that are true. However, while the doctrine that actions are explained by choices self-referentially and causally is the point of departure of Aristotelian theories, it is not their destination. In recognizing choice as the essential element in human action, their object is to explain it by explaining choices. As we have seen, they go on to explain choices by wishes and by intentions formed by deliberation. A choice is an intention to perform a specific action, as the immediate step to be taken in carrying out a plan, perhaps a highly complex one, that is directed at bringing about a wished for end. How do those wishes and deliberations produce plans, and how do those plans explain choices? Remembering our principle, that the reasonableness of a reason cannot by itself explain why it is acted on, once again we must look for a causal factor. But where?

Let us begin with an example simpler than any I have so far considered: it is adapted from one of Stoutland's.

> You intend to get rid of a bat if you acceptably can.
> You believe that you can acceptably get rid of it if you open a door and stand away from it.
> Therefore, you open a door and stand away from it.

Plainly, your intention and belief do not logically require you to choose to do what you do; for there are other ways of getting rid of bats, such as catching them in newspaper, or in a net, which you may be aware of and prefer.

It is tempting to strengthen the belief premise. For example, to amend it to:

> You believe that you can acceptably get rid of the bat if and only if you open a door and stand away from it.

This temptation should be resisted. Sometimes, it is true, premises as strong as this are available, but more often they are not; and an analysis that applies to all cases is needed. For similar reasons, a variation suggested by Aristotle should be avoided also, namely:

> You believe that the best way you can get rid of the bat is to open a door and stand away from it.

Sometimes such a premise is available, but often it is not. Human beings do not act only when they believe that they are acting either in the one and only way to bring about what they wish, or in the best way.

As I have argued in chapter 3, if your practical reasoning follows normal lines, the explanation of what you do will contain an additional question and answer, namely:

> You ask yourself, 'Is that good enough as a solution of the problem, or do I need to investigate what others there may be?' and you answer, 'Yes, it's good enough, there is no need for me to deliberate further.'

If you give yourself that answer, then, given that you intend to get rid of the bat as soon as you have decided how you acceptably can, you would be inconsistent, if you continue both to have that intention to hold those beliefs, not to choose to open a door and stand away from it.

At this point, the difficulty with which we began recurs: namely, that the fact that a reason is good does not explain why we act on it. Yes, it would be inconsistent to have the intention and the beliefs you have, and yet not to choose to open the door and stand away from it. But are you always consistent? Is anybody?

The solution may be found in many philosophers, of whom I single out Aquinas and Descartes, both of whom resort to the metaphor of light. According to Aquinas,

> with respect to [its object], two acts of reason come under consideration. First of all, as it apprehends the truth about something. This is not in our power; for it happens by virtue of some light, whether natural or supernatural. The other act of reason is when it assents to what it apprehends. If, however, things should be apprehended to which the intellect naturally assents, assent to them or dissent from them is not in our power, but in the order of nature. . . . Things are, however, apprehended which do not thus convince the intellect, rather it

can assent or dissent, or at least can suspend assent or dissent
on some ground or other. In such cases, assent or dissent is in
our power, and falls under [our] command (Aquinas (1), I–II,
17, 6).

Descartes, in a parallel observation, affirms that, even in the
first case, the will remains free. I cannot but judge that some
things I understand very clearly are true, he wrote, 'not
because I [am] compelled so to judge by any external force,
but because a great light in the intellect [is] followed by a great
inclination in the will, and thus the spontaneity and freedom of
my belief [is] all the greater in proportion to my lack of
indifference.' When confronted with the light of my understanding that 'from the very fact of my raising [the] question
[whether anything in the world exists] it follows quite evident-
ly that I exist,' my will, by its own nature, is caused to judge
that it does so follow (Descartes, VII, 58–9).

The causal property on which Aristotelian explanations of
human choice rest is the capacity to perceive elementary
irrationality, and the will to reject it. Given that normal
human adults on most occasions exhibit this property, then for
the most part, not only can their choices be explained by their
wishes and by the intentions produced from them by their
deliberations, but the conclusions of their deliberations can be
explained by their other beliefs. That not all human behaviour
can be so explained is not an objection; for practical reason in
anybody can malfunction in conditions of extreme physical or
mental injury or stress; and when it does, behaviour results
that is not explicable as human action, but rather as its
breakdown.

Yet doubts remain about the soundness of the grounds on
which those Aristotelians for whom Aquinas and Descartes
speak ascribe this causal property to normal human adults.
Obviously both Aquinas and Descartes took themselves as
representative, and thought it enough to report on the conditions in which assent or dissent was in their power, and those

in which it was not (according to Descartes, without any restriction of freedom). There are elementary cases in which they concluded that the light is too strong for there to be any option, or for it to be possible to wish for an option. But do all human beings share that light? If they do, how can it be established?

Not only would empirical surveys be inconclusive as well as impracticable, it is hard to get rid of the suspicion that there has to be a theoretical reason for what Aquinas and Descartes assert. And Descartes's famous joke, 'Good sense is the best distributed thing in the world: for everyone thinks himself so well endowed with it that even those who are the hardest to please in everything else do not desire more of it than they have' (Descartes, VI, 2), suggests that he had some inkling of that reason. It is bad manners not to treat your fellows as being possessed of good sense. But is it not more than bad manners? Can human beings have practical relations with one another on any other terms than crediting one another with the capacity to perceive elementary irrationality, and the will to reject it?

Our practical relations with one another depend on our capacity to explain our behaviour by ascribing propositional attitudes to one another. Ascribing to you belief both in a proposition and in its contradictory would make it impossible to form any coherent notion of what you believe with respect to either. And describing you, on one hand, as taking an appetitive attitude to the bringing about of a certain end by some acceptable means, and on the other, as withholding an appetitive attitude towards the only acceptable means you consider worth inquiring into, would make it impossible to form any coherent notion of your appetitive attitudes towards that means. Of course, if we do not form coherent notions of one another's cognitive and appetitive attitudes, we cannot explain one another's behaviour at all.

Well, can we? To this the only possible answer is that

ordinary human intercourse is nothing other than behaving as though we do. Seriously to doubt that we do, and at the same time to behave as though we do, would be not only an extraordinary feat of accommodation to cognitive dissonance, but one that promises no intellectual profit.

In the example given, in view of your intention to get rid of a bat if you acceptably can, and your beliefs that you can get rid of it by opening a door and standing aside, and that there is no need to inquire into other ways of doing it, you cannot consistently not choose to open a door and stand aside. Nor, if you are a normal human adult, can you be inconsistent in cases so elementary. For in them, if you cannot recognize that you must either make a choice, or abandon either a belief or the intention that set you deliberating, you cannot coherently be credited with beliefs and intentions of all. The lapses that occur in special circumstances for example, those in which you are under great stress, confirm the soundness of the Socratic tradition. For to the extent that you lose your grip on elementary consistency, you cease to be able to deliberate, and hence to choose. You can only be described as acting, as distinct from doing things over which you have no control, if you retain the power to notice your condition, and to refrain from initiating anything on the matters on which you have lost control.

CHAPTER 8

WILL AND INTELLECT

What does the theory of action developed in the preceding chapters imply about who and what we are? Most obviously, that we are creatures not merely of desire, but also of will.

It is non-controversial that the behaviour of non-rational animals – those of species the normal members of which do not, with normal nurture, acquire the capacity to take propositional attitudes – cannot be explained by their cognitive capacities, sensation and imagination, alone. They must also have an appetitive capacity, the objects of which are also objects of their cognitive capacities. And the actualizations of that capacity, if such animals are aware of them at all, will themselves be objects of sense as felt attractions and repulsions. Appetites their possessors can feel, that are elicited by objects that are sensed or imagined, are varieties of what Aristotle called *epithumia* or desire.

Rational creatures, who are capable of cognitive propositional attitudes as well as of sensation and imagination, thereby have a more extensive range of desires; for they are immediately attracted to or repelled by some of the possibilities they think of as well as by some of those they sense or imagine, and can feel those attractions and repulsions. Smelling the roast in the oven, you may hunger for some of it just as your dog may, without benefit of any proposition; but thinking that righteousness is comely, which your dog cannot, you may hunger for that also.

A dog, attracted by a poisoned bait, and summoned away from it by its master's voice, has conflicting desires, and does whatever he imagines will put him in the imagined situation that attracts him more: the one in which his master's summons is not disregarded, or the one in which he eats the bait. One attraction of what is imagined overpowers the other, perhaps after some vacillation. By contrast, according to the overwhelming preponderance of what is said and presumably thought about them, conflicts of desires in human beings are seldom settled like that. Which of a set of conflicting desires a human being chooses to act on is not simply a matter of their strength, considered as something that can be felt, but rather a matter of which he wishes most to act on. Sometimes the two coincide. When you thirst for a cup of the coffee you smell in the pot before you, you will wish to satisfy that thirst; and as long as that wish conflicts only with wishes to gratify other and weaker desires, such as not to trouble yourself to pour a cup, what you will wish most to act on will presumably be your wish to gratify your strongest desire, and you will therefore choose to pour and drink a cup.

Sometimes, however, your strongest wish does not coincide with your strongest desire. Not all wishes are to gratify desires. We all wish to bring about all sorts of things about which we feel nothing at all, as well as to bring about things we desire; and they may be the wishes we elect to gratify. You long to leave your office, go home, and relax with a martini; and yet you have an appointment to keep, keeping which is not a means to something else you desire, and of which the very thought sickens you. Even so, for different motives on different occasions, you sometimes choose to forgo the escape you long for, and to keep the appointment you shrink from. This well-attested fact, which underlies the entire Socratic tradition, compels us to postulate an appetitive capacity besides desire: an intellectual capacity that not only can be directed to propositional objects, but which is related to desire as thinking is related to sensation. This is the capacity that the medieval Aristotelians called '*voluntas*' (in English, 'will'), in defining which they appropriated Aristotle's description of choice: namely, 'rational appetite'.

Many philosophers recoil when confronted with the empirical grounds for recognizing this capacity (cf. Hornsby, 46–58). Even Davidson, in the very paper in which he showed that intentions are propositional attitudes distinct from desires, refused to consider any theory that identified intending something with 'any mysterious act of will or special attitude or episode of willing' (Davidson (1), 87, cf. 101). It did not occur to him to doubt that, if there were acts of will, they would be 'mysterious'. Yet why would they be? Why should intending something not be an episode of taking a special attitude, namely willing, to some proposition?

Ever since Hume declared that all the contents of the mind are perceptions, philosophers have divided into two parties. On one side, his followers dismissed as medieval mystifications all alleged mental attitudes or episodes that they could not persuade themselves are reducible to perceptions. It is true that, had their powers of self-persuasion with regard to their reductions of the cognitive powers not been truly formidable, they could never have imagined that any of their theories was acceptable. On the other side, non-Humeans had little difficulty in showing that Humean reductions of the cognitive powers are false: that, for example, whatever a belief may be, it is not a vivid image. But they were less assured in their treatment of the appetitive powers.

Here Kant's influence was unfortunate. For while he held that there are acts of will, he agreed with Hume that they have no place in the phenomenal realm of either outer or inner sense: either in the starry heavens above, or in the flow of consciousness within, both inexorably governed by the laws of nature. They belong in the noumenal realm that is beyond space and time, and which is feebly governed by the moral law. It cannot be denied that if they belong there, they are mysterious indeed. If postulating a noumenal realm distinct from that which our senses disclose to us is the only way of saving the pre-Humean theory of will, then few will choose to save it, even among philosophers who are unpersuaded by Hume. But there is no need to postulate such a realm. Kant's moral theory can be detached from the transcendental idealism by which he offered to show how natural science is possible, and it should be. When it is thus detached, the theory of action it incorporates can be seen as what it is: a revival of the traditional pre-Humean one.

Yet the attitudes and episodes the existence of which Hume denied have never ceased to haunt the work of his successors. For, if desire is the only appetitive power that can be treated on Humean lines, the decisive empirical objections to reducing intention to desire show that an acceptable theory of the appetitive propositional attitudes will be non-Humean. And willy-nilly such theories are apt to resemble the pre-Humean ones.

Two obstacles to recognizing that there are appetitive propositional attitudes can be identified and removed. The first is the lingering conception of the realm of the mental as a flux of consciousness or 'experience'. The realm of the mental, as Ryle recognized, is that of certain human powers or capacities, and of their exercise. Those powers or capacities divide into two, the sensory-imaginative, and the intellectual. Neither kind is a mystery in any philosophically useful sense. Normal adults not only exercise both kinds every day of their lives, but also interpret one another's behaviour in terms of a large and sophisticated set of concepts of capacities of both kinds. Nor is there anything mysterious about these concepts, as they are commonly employed. What has made there appear to be is the Humean philosophy itself: it is indeed a mystery how to interpret our mental life as a flux of Humean perceptions.

The second obstacle to be removed is suspicion of any concept of power or causality that cannot be analysed in terms of observable regularities. Astonishingly, until Anscombe pointed it out, very few philosophers in the analytic tradition recognized that most of the causal vocabulary in which physical events are customarily described cannot be so analysed, or drew the obvious conclusion that what is sauce for the physical goose is sauce for the mental gander.

By the latter half of the twentieth century, most analytical philosophers followed Russell in thinking of beliefs as propositional attitudes. From a Humean point of view, this is utterly mysterious. For the propositional objects of beliefs need not appear before consciousness as remotely like Humean perceptions – for example, as imagined sentences, or as mental pictures. And, if everything mental that is not an item in the flow of consciousness is ghostly, the attitude of believing itself – that of holding the proposition to which it is directed to be true – is equally suspect. Yet what in our mental life is less mysterious than holding propositions to be true? Ryle was, I think, quite right when he treated beliefs as far less mysterious than phenomena like after-images, the Humean credentials of which are impeccable. We know how to express beliefs. We make very few mistakes about whether or not we believe this proposition or that. And, as a matter of course, we explain much in our own and others' behaviour by reference to what we and they believe and intend.

On the face of it, it is puzzling why philosophers who find beliefs acceptably unmysterious should not find intentions and choices so as well. Since they countenance beliefs, they cannot scruple at takings of propositional attitudes as such. Why then discriminate between those that are acts of will and those that are acts of intellect?

One reason is that they doubt whether putative acts of will are expressible in speech. If, as has been assumed throughout the present investigation, propositional attitudes are characteristically expressible in speech, then any such attitude that appeared not to be thus expressible would be suspect. In this respect, there is no controversy about beliefs. You can express any of your beliefs, say, your belief that you are wearing black socks, by uttering a sentence expressing the proposition you believe, in this case, 'I am wearing black socks'; for any utterance expressing a proposition has the sense that its truth-conditions are satisfied. By contrast, those who agree that wishes, intentions and choices are propositional attitudes have found it difficult to agree about how they are to be expressed. And to the extent that serious reasons for disagreement persist, what is disagreed about remains obscure at least.

For one appetitive propositional attitude, namely wishing, there is no difficulty. Most natural languages have optative constructions. Just as 'I shall wear black socks tomorrow' expresses a belief, so 'Would that I wear black socks tomorrow' expresses a wish. Intentions and choices, however, are another matter; for they go beyond wishing in being peremptory.

While you can wish to wear black socks tomorrow without expecting to be able to do so, or having it in mind to do anything to bring it about that you do so, you cannot intend or choose to wear black socks tomorrow without having in mind to do something about it. When you put black socks on, you carry out what you have in mind; and carrying out what you have in mind bears some resemblance to obeying a command. May this not be a clue? If intending resembles commanding, then perhaps intending that something be done can be expressed in the same way as commanding it, by uttering a sentence in the imperative mood expressing it.

Both R.M. Hare and Anthony Kenny have embraced this conclusion, although neither has made much of the distinction between optative and imperative forms. Both intending that something be done and commanding it, they argue, are expressible by uttering sentences in the imperative mood expressing the proposition to which those attitudes are taken. For example, you can express your intention to wear black socks tomorrow by saying to yourself as you go to bed: 'Now wear black socks tomorrow!' (Kenny (2), 29–35).

It has been objected that Hare and Kenny confound forming intentions with addressing commands to yourself. They rightly deny it. Their position is that the imperative mood can be used to express prescriptions of any variety, and not commands only. But if the imperative mood can express prescriptions of any kind, how can it express intentions as distinct from other prescriptions, for example, self-addressed commands? As a commanding officer, you have issued the command that all ranks are to wear black socks tomorrow. As you go to bed saying to yourself, 'Black socks tomorrow!' how do you distinguish whether you are expressing an intention or addressing a command to yourself? After all, you may be planning to desert in the early hours, and be amusing yourself with a self-addressed command you have no intention of obeying.

If the imperative mood can be used to express any prescription, it follows that no specific sort of prescription is expressed simply by uttering a sentence in the imperative mood stating what is to be done: different species of prescription will be discriminated from one another by something over and above that. Nor will it help to invent artificial locutions by which to do it, unless those locutions can be expressed in the language we already speak. Artificial notations are properly introduced to display clearly the unformulated conventions by which we interpret what we say to one another. Frege's and Russell's notations for quantification are an example: they displayed clearly for the first time what is involved in distinctions we draw without difficulty in speaking to one another, such as that between 'Every boy loves some girl', and 'There is some girl that every boy loves'.

If in speaking to one another we distinguish between

imperative utterances expressing self-addressed commands and those expressing intentions, how do we do it? Since *ex hypothesi* it is not by any difference in the sentences we utter, presumably it is by some difference in the circumstances in which they are uttered. And since a variety of prescriptive speech acts can be addressed to yourself, that you are talking to yourself cannot be the circumstance by which one is distinguished from the others.

The circumstance that a command is self-addressed does not suffice to make it an expression of an intention, or even of a wish; for you can intend to disobey a command you address to yourself. Moreover, imperatives are commands addressed to somebody who is to obey them. Intending therefore seems to belong with obeying rather than with commanding. For that reason, the relation which the medieval Aristotelians identified with that of commanding was that between intellect and will, not that between will and what they called the 'executive powers' (cf. Aquinas (1), I–II, 17, 1 and 5). Acts of will presuppose power to execute, not legitimate authority that may be flouted. In intending you do not command your body and mind to obey you, as though you are an authority your mind and body may conceivably disobey. Rather, you presuppose that your intending will self-referentially cause what you intend to come about. You exercise your power to move your body and mind, within certain limits, as you choose. If you fail to do what you intend, it is not because your body or mind are disobedient, but because you lack the power you presuppose you have.

If you will to exercise such a presupposed power, how can you express your willing it? Searle has supplied what is needed for an answer, although the question matters little to him, believing as he does that some animals can wish, intend, deliberate and choose even though they cannot express those attitudes in speech. It is that intentions are expressed by the same linguistic forms as beliefs, and that expressions of intention differ from expressions of belief only in the direction of fit their speakers treat them as having. 'I shall get up at six tomorrow morning' can be used to express either a belief or an intention. Since fitting in one direction rather than another is not a semantic property, the direction of fit you treat such an utterance as having cannot be part of the sense of what you utter. Nor can prefixing a clause in which your attitude is specified; for that can be no more than an expression of belief. In saying, 'Yes, I intend that I shall get up at six tomorrow morning', you may not be undertaking to do anything, but merely describing your present state of mind. Hence you may be disbelieved without imputing dishonesty to you. We can be deceived about whether we are persisting in an intention (cf. Searle (1), 166–75).

The direction of fit of an utterance is shown for the most part by its context, both linguistic and non-linguistic. There is nothing any of us can do to affect the truth or falsity of most of the sentences we utter: all those about the past, for example. But sentences about the future of which the truth or falsity depends on what the speaker will do may obviously have world-to-mind direction of fit. Accompanying expressions of attitude can also serve as guides, although ambiguously. 'I shall get up at six in the morning tomorrow – I've done so for twenty years' does not normally express an intention; but 'I shall get up at six in the morning tomorrow – I shall! I shall!' normally does. Unlike the former, the latter is true only if you intend to get up at six; but it also implies that if you persist in what you intend, and presuppose nothing false in intending it, you will get up then. You can also indicate the attitude you are expressing to a proposition by adding to your expression of it a description of what you are expressing.

If this is correct, then wishes, intentions and choices are all expressible in speech as readily as beliefs, although by expressions that, apart from their contexts, are ambiguous.

Are there any other reasons why philosophers who dismiss

Humean objections to cognitive propositional attitudes should regard appetitive attitudes like wishes, intentions and choices as mysterious? One reason might be that they are superfluous. There is some support in the Aristotelian tradition itself for thinking that they are, and more in its Socratic sources. Choices and intentions are appetitive attitudes explained by deliberation and the non-deliberative appetitive attitude of wishing. Yet what human beings wish for is not determined by their nature as human: different human beings wish for different things. Why? Most Aristotelians answer: because they have different beliefs about what the non-instrumental human good is.

All agree that it is a condition called by Aristotle sometimes *eudaimonia* and sometimes *to makarion*, and by Aquinas sometimes *felicitas* and sometimes *beatitudo*. The usual English translations are 'happiness' and 'blessedness'. And all agree that this condition is variously identified: as pleasure, as riches, as honour, and as activity according to human excellence in a complete life. To those the medieval Aristotelians added a supernatural option, the beatific vision of God. Which of these conditions, if any, is *eudaimonia*, is a matter of indifference to action theory, but not the doctrine that wishes arise from beliefs about what the human good is. For if they do, then appetitive attitudes are no more than intermediate causes of human actions; and intermediate causes are apt to be jettisoned as idle.

There is, however, a difficulty. Human beings do not consistently wish for what they believe to be the human good. True, they never prefer what they believe to be outright evil to what they believe to be good: they wish only *sub specie boni*. But they sometimes prefer what they believe to have some good in it to what they believe is a greater good. That is, they exhibit what Aristotle called *akrasia*, or incontinence. To take one of Aristotle's examples, you may believe that there are ridiculous things it is bad to do no matter for whose sake, and yet, like

Satyrus nicknamed 'the filial', do them out of devotion to your father and be 'thought very silly on this point' (Aristotle (4), VII, 1148b 1–2).

Aristotle himself refused to describe Satyrus as an *akrates*, or incontinent man, on the ground that although his excess was 'bad and to be avoided', it is not 'worthy of blame' (Aristotle (4), VII, 1148b 3–6). And most philosophers have followed him in eschewing expressions equivalent to *akrasia* and its cognates when describing actions that are not immoral. Yet the phenomenon that matters for action theory is going against one's own judgement of what is better than what. What chiefly matters for ethical theory, namely, going against true judgements of it, is something entirely different; and the two ought not to be yoked together by violence. I shall therefore use the word 'incontinence' to express the concept needed by action theory, namely, that of acting against one's own judgement of the human good, irrespective of whether it is true or false. Davidson's advice is worth following: 'In approaching the problem of incontinence it is a good idea to dwell on the cases where morality simply doesn't enter the picture as one of the contestants for our favour – or if it does, it is on the wrong side' (Davidson (1), 30).

The obvious explanation of incontinence is that believing that a proposed end has some good in it, while a necessary condition of wishing that it be brought about, is not a sufficient one. Nor is it sufficient that among the potential ends you believe to be attainable and good, there is one you believe to be the best. If wishing to bring about (or intending) is in this way an ultimate cause of action, not one that is merely intermediate, incontinent wishing is possible.

Yet few Aristotelians are prepared to leave it at that. Aristotle himself distinguishes two kinds of incontinence, weakness (*astheneia*) and impetuosity (*propeteia*).

> For some men [he writes] after deliberating fail, owing to their passion, to stand by the conclusions of their deliberation, others

because they have not deliberated are led by their passion
(Aristotle (4), VII, 1150b 19–22).

In each case, he attributes their incontinence, not to their
ceasing to wish to make true the proposition that is the major
premise laying down the end deliberated about, but either to
their not choosing according to the conclusion reached (weakness), or to their not carrying their deliberation through
(impetuosity). And he puts both failures down to passion.
Because of passion, although they either reach a correct
conclusion, or accept premises that would enable them to
reach it, they do so as a drunkard or somebody half-asleep
does: they do not fully believe either the conclusion or that
there is a conclusion to be drawn (cf. Aristotle (4), VII, 1147a
6–18). As Kenny admirably puts it, Aristotle holds that the
incontinent man only 'half has' either the conclusion of his
deliberation, or any awareness that a conclusion can be drawn
(Kenny (3), 162–3).

The objection to Aristotle's explanation is that, while cases
of the kinds he describes as weakness and impetuosity are
undoubtedly found, those of neither kind appear to be full
human actions. In neither, as Davidson has pointed out,

> is it . . . clear how we can ever blame the agent for what he
> does: his action merely reflects the outcome of a struggle within
> him. What could he do about it? And more important, the first
> image does not allow us to make sense of a conflict in one
> person's soul, for it leaves no room for the all-important process
> of weighing considerations (Davidson (1), 35–6).

To obtain cases of incontinent actions, as distinct from behaviour in which the agent's passions have overcome his
power to control what he does, a process of weighing must be
postulated, and that process can occur only if the agent has the
capacity to carry it out. And if that capacity is not one of
forming beliefs, what can it be except one that is appetitive?

At this point Davidson has supplied the solution that eluded both Aristotle himself, and the medieval Aristotelians. It presupposes three things. First, that there are two kinds of proposition about the human good that can be believed: those that are *prima facie* or 'as far as they go' beliefs, and those that are 'all out'. Secondly, that deliberation is from 'as far as they go' premises to 'all out' conclusions, and is therefore never strictly deductive. And thirdly, that 'all out' conclusions are rationally drawn only from intermediate conclusions about what is so in view of 'all things considered'. Propositions about what, all things considered, is good or right are a variety of 'as far as they go' propositions; for all the things that are considered are seldom all that there are. Given these presuppositions, an incontinent man can be defined as somebody who, having arrived by deliberation at a belief about what 'all things considered' it would be best to do, nevertheless believes that it is 'all out' best to do something else, and so acts accordingly.

Davidson takes the following example from Aquinas. Somebody believes the teaching of the Church that what is contrary to divine law is 'all things considered' worse than anything that is not, and that fornication is contrary to the divine law. But he also believes that pleasure is good 'as far as it goes', and that a particular fornication for which he has an opportunity would be a very great pleasure. Weighing up these two pieces of practical reasoning, he decides that it is best, 'all out', to fornicate. He does not reason inconsistently; for no inference to an 'all out' conclusion from 'as far as it goes' premises is logically necessary, even from those of the 'all things considered' variety. Yet he does reason irrationally; for a principle of practical reasoning that it would be irrational not to adopt is: 'perform the action judged best on the basis of all available relevant reasons' (Davidson (1), 41).

We now can explain the phenomenon of incontinence without invoking any appetitive attitude that is not intermediate. How can somebody who believes that something is for the best nevertheless choose to do something else, and yet never act except out of a wish for what he believes to be for the best? Because there are two relevant senses in which something can be believed to be for the best: 'all things considered' and 'all out'. An incontinent man believes that something is for the best in the former sense, and yet chooses to act on his belief that something else is for the best in the latter sense. And such choices are incontinent because, while consistent, they violate a principle of practical reasoning which it is irrational not to observe.

Figure I sets out how Aristotelians would analyse Socrates' explanation of why he remained in prison. His action is immediately caused by his taking an appetitive attitude of

FIGURE I

BELIEFS (*DOXAI*)	APPETITIVE ATTI-TUDES (*OREXES*)
Socrates believes that anybody's highest good is the good of his city, his city being Athens.	Socrates wishes for the good of his city, Athens.
Socrates deliberates how best to promote the good of Athens, and concludes that it requires obedience to Athenian law.	Socrates intends to promote the good of Athens by obeying Athenian law.
Socrates concludes further that obeying Athenian law requires him to remain in prison and submit to his sentence.	Socrates chooses to remain in prison and submit to his sentence (with the intention of promoting the good of his city, Athens).

choice, which is preceded by his taking appetitive attitudes of intending and wishing. But each of these appetitive attitudes is taken because of a counterpart belief. Davidson has seen that any such analysis invites us to ask whether postulating such appetitive attitudes does any work. Can the whole analysis not be simplified by dispensing with them, and explaining Socrates' action purely by their counterpart beliefs? His explanation of incontinence shows how they can be dispensed with.

This is how to do it. First, identify the first two appetitive attitudes (a wish and a not fully determinate intention) with their counterpart evaluative beliefs, which, being about the highest good, are 'all things considered' beliefs. Secondly, treat the third appetitive attitude (a choice) as a mingling of two

FIGURE II

EVALUATIVE JUDGEMENTS (*DOXAI*)

[Wish]

Socrates believes that, all things considered, his highest good is the same as everybody's: the good of his city, namely, Athens.

[Conditional intentions]

As a result of deliberation, Socrates believes that, all things considered, by obeying Athenian law, and only by that, can he in his situation promote his highest good, the good of Athens.

As a result of deliberating about what obeying Athenian law requires, and of surveying the results of his other deliberations, Socrates believes that, all things considered, the best thing for him to do is to remain in prison and submit to his sentence.

[Choice, or unconditional intention]

Socrates believes that, all out, the best thing for him to do is to remain in prison and submit to his sentence.

beliefs that need to be distinguished: first, its Aristotelian counterpart, also an 'all things considered' belief; and secondly, a corresponding 'all out' belief. This belief is Socrates' fully determinate intention or choice, by which his remaining in prison and submitting to his sentence is explained.

The result of Davidson's Socratic simplification of Aristotle's analysis is represented in Figure II. Aristotle and his medieval followers pair each of the appetitive attitudes they recognize with a belief about what is good, because they believe, as Aquinas put it, that 'in the manner of a formal cause . . . the intellect moves the will by presenting its object to it' (Aquinas (1), I–1II, 9, 1). If that were so, then the case for Davidson's simplification would be irresistible. For if each and every *orexis* were explained by a counterpart *doxa* about what is for the best, then everything that it explains could be explained by that counterpart without its mediation. And if those *orexes* are discarded as superfluous, what have been taken to be varieties (wishes, intentions, choices) of a distinct appetitive kind of propositional attitude are revealed to be varieties of the familiar cognitive attitude of belief to propositions of a specific kind (propositions about what is good), arising from differences of mode (in how it is said to be good – 'all things considered' or 'all out') and of the sort of good referred to (good as end and good as means).

Whether Davidson's simplification is sound turns on whether or not there are choices that cannot be identified with all out evaluative beliefs. Unfortunately for it, Bratman has found a class of such choices. They arise out of what he has described as 'an analogue of the old problem of Buridan's Ass' (Bratman (2), 22–3). You wish to drop in at a bookstore on your way home; two are convenient, both of which you patronize, and neither of which do you prefer to the other: so you choose one by flipping a coin. Can such a choice be described as a belief that all out the one you choose is better than the other? Davidson argues as follows that it can.

[I]f there is reason to reach some decision, and there are no obvious or intrinsic grounds for decision, we find extrinsic grounds. Perhaps I flip a coin to decide. My need to choose has caused me to prefer the alternative indicated by the toss; a trivial ground for preference, but a good enough one in the absence of others (Davidson (3), 200).

This, however, overlooks that Bratman's difficulty is only an analogue of Buridan's. It is not, as Buridan's was, 'How does the ass decide?' Nobody denies that you, unlike the ass, decide by finding an extrinsic ground. Rather it is that accepting a ground that is extrinsic cannot be the same as believing that all out the alternative chosen is better than the other. That it can be rational to choose on extrinsic grounds shows that there can be choices without all out value judgements.

Buridan's Ass, being what he was, could not solve the problem of how to decide between two alternatives which he judged all out to be better than any others, but equally good. He had not the wit to perceive that, since he has a reason to choose (namely, that he wants his luncheon) even though he does not believe that all out one is better than the other, he has reason to choose on an extrinsic ground. Such choices themselves may be rational or irrational: it is irrational, for example, to choose on a ground that is inconvenient. But usually several will be equally convenient. Whether a coin falls heads or tails is an extrinsic ground that will usually not be all out better than whether a straw drawn is longer or shorter.

Nevertheless, the weight of the Aristotelian tradition is on Davidson's side. Why? I suspect that it is because of a temptation to which he himself has drawn attention, and against which he has warned us: the temptation to moralize choice, or at least to imagine that there is always a rational standard by which any choice must be better or worse than its alternatives. It is the temptation to think of most people's lives as more colourful than they are. Evelyn Waugh's Mr Pinfold 'would look at his watch and learn always with disappointment how little of his life was past, how much there was still ahead of him.' What remained would confront him with choices, but with few that would make much difference to himself or anybody else. Nor need such a prospect make for unhappiness. You may be perfectly content that the larger features of your future life seem fixed, as long as none of your options in lesser matters are repugnant.

Humdrum lives may abound in petty choices. For that reason, they also abound in non-controversial examples of appetitive propositional attitudes which there is no temptation to confound with beliefs about what is all out for the best. Unless this evidence can be impugned, purely appetitive propositional attitudes cannot be eliminated in favour of beliefs about what is all out for the best.

Yet in cases in which one of the options under consideration is believed to be all out for the best, must not what is chosen accord with that belief? If it could be established that it must, then Davidson's analysis of incontinence could be retained, even though his elimination of appetitive propositional attitudes cannot. Unfortunately, since there are cases in which human beings choose between options without believing that one is all out better than the others, it can be established only if it can be ascertained, independently of its being chosen, whether or not an option is believed to be all out for the best. Since Davidson arrived at his analysis by investigating how actions are explained, and not by studying what people do or avow, I do not think he would claim that this can be ascertained. And if it cannot, it is economical to explain in the same way both choices among options believed equally good, and choices of options believed worse than others that are available: namely, as exercises of an intellectual appetitive power that is not confined to options believed to be best. When somebody making a choice believes either that he has several equally good options, or that he has better options than the one he chooses, to postulate a mediating all out value judgement between his belief and his choice would be theoretically idle.

Irrational all out value judgements are no more explicable than irrational intellectual appetitive attitudes. It would be defensible to postulate them, on grounds of economy, if weakness of will were the only phenomenon which an intellectual appetitive power serves to explain. But if such attitudes are needed to explain choices between indifferent alternatives, the argument from economy is reversed. There is now no need to postulate all out value judgements. The phenomena they are introduced to explain can be explained by attitudes there is independent reason to accept: appetitive intellectual attitudes that are not confined to options that are believed to be the best.

Weakness of will is therefore just that: weakness in taking appetitive intellectual attitudes to options that are believed, all things considered, to be the best. It is possible for you to intend to bring about some end you judge good by carrying out a certain plan, and then, for some other end you judge good but less good, to abandon your intention and choose to do something else. You have not formed an irrational belief about which of the two is all out better. On the contrary, you have taken an irrational appetitive attitude – you have renounced an end you judge better for one you judge worse. It is true that you have a reason, but a reason you judge not good enough.

To sum up. If there are formings of appetitive intellectual propositional attitudes, persistings in them, and abandonings of them, then human beings must have the capacity to engage in those formings, persistings and abandonings. And that capacity cannot be the same as the capacity to form, to persist in, and to abandon beliefs, questions and other cognitive attitudes. It is therefore necessary to distinguish two rational capacities in human beings: one that is exercised in taking cognitive propositional attitudes (usually named 'the intellect'), and another that is exercised in taking appetitive intellectual ones (for which nobody has proposed a better name than its old one, 'the will'). Neither intellect nor will, so understood, is a substance, or an homunculus. Each is a human power or capacity. If their exercises are mysterious, what characteristic human activity is not? And if they are not mysterious, then the capacities of which they are the exercises are not mysterious either.

CHAPTER 9

AGENCY

Taking a propositional attitude is not, in primitive cases, an action. A child is capable of believing, wishing and intending if he has developed sufficiently (1) to wish for an end, say to relieve an unpleasant feeling in his arms; (2) to form beliefs, such as that stretching them will relieve that feeling, and that he can stretch them; and (3), given no other wish he believes will be frustrated if he stretches them, to intend to stretch them. And the result of his so wishing, believing and intending will be that he does stretch them, if he is right in believing that he can. At this early stage of his development, his wishing, believing and intending are not in turn explained by further wishes, beliefs and intentions; for, since he has as yet no concepts of wishing, believing or intending, he cannot think about his wishes, beliefs and intentions at all.

Any taking of a propositional attitude that is not itself explained by its taker's intending to take it was described by the medieval Aristotelians as 'elicited' and not 'commanded' (cf. Aquinas (1), I–II, 1, 1 *ad* 2). Such takings of propositional attitudes, 'elicited' without being explained by any further intentions, are spontaneous exercises of their takers' capacities of intellect and will. The earliest action each human being performs are explained by their earliest and most primitive exercises of those capacities. Those primitive actions are presumably bodily, because bits of bodily behaviour may be presumed to be the objects of their earliest beliefs about their powers.

As human beings mature, they acquire from their elders concepts of such propositional attitudes as believing, wishing and intending. Which they acquire will depend on their cultures; but whatever their culture may be, they will acquire some. When they do, they can form beliefs about their own mental lives, and, most importantly, beliefs about which events in their mental lives depend upon spontaneous exercises of their mental capacities. Having formed such beliefs, they are in a position to take appetitive attitudes to such events, and in particular, to intend that they bring about this one or that. According to the analysis of human action developed in the previous chapters, any taking of a propositional attitude that is self-referentially brought about by its taker's intending (choosing) to take it is a mental action. It can be assumed that human beings in every culture have the concept of belief, and some concepts of appetitive propositional attitude. They may not have the concepts of intending or choosing. It follows that they may not be able to intend to intend, or to choose to choose; but they will be able to form intentions and to make choices about the cognitive and appetitive propositional attitudes of which they do have concepts. The capacity to intend and choose does not depend on having the concepts of intending and choosing.

Perhaps nobody has ever seriously questioned that the takings of attitudes that constitute calculating or deliberating can be intended or chosen, and hence full human actions; but some mental actions are much simpler. Anybody who only has beliefs but thinks of himself as having them, and wonders which of them he should continue to have, presumably wishes to persist in some of them (such as that he has good manners) but not in others (such as that he is sometimes ridiculous), and at the same time to do so intelligently. In some cases, such wishes will be idle. You may wish, like Hobbes, to believe that you have solved the problem of squaring the circle; but if you understand the proof that it cannot be done, as Hobbes did not, you cannot avoid believing that what you wish to believe is false. Most beliefs, however, are not like that.

Consider the case of Othello in Shakespeare's play. He is told by Iago that his lieutenant, Cassio, has blabbed that he has slept with Othello's wife, Desdemona; Desdemona tells him that Cassio has not done so. Whom is Othello to believe? Although it is a precept of common morality that husbands ought to trust their wives unless they are proved untrustworthy, Othello, blind to his proneness to jealousy, believes Iago. Later, it is true, he denounced himself as a 'gull, [a] dolt, as ignorant as dirt'. But was he to blame? If believing or disbelieving cannot be an action, then he was not. O'Shaughnessy has argued that, since believing is accepting as true, you cannot believe something on a ground (such as a common moral precept) that you acknowledge may lead you to accept something false as true (O'Shaughnessy, I, 25). Examples like that of Othello call such arguments in question. No doubt Othello cannot wholly control his imagination, or suppress his suspicions. But he can accept Desdemona's denial as true in all his plans of action.

The duty to his wife in which Othello fails is not that he trust her unless the weight of evidence is against her. Such evidence as he has was fabricated by Iago: and its weight, although far from decisive, is against her. What is wrong with O'Shaughnessy's plausible argument is that in many fields, both theoretical and practical, any defensible procedure you can follow in fixing your beliefs will sometimes lead you into error; and in some of those fields, it is right to allow considerations not directly connected with truth and falsity to affect what procedure you decide on, for example, that you owe somebody trust. What Othello and Desdemona owe one another as husband and wife cannot make a difference to what either of them believes about evident truths regarding which they are adequately informed; but it can and ought to make a difference to how each receives evidence that is less than conclusive for imputations against the other.

If Othello were to accept Desdemona's word, despite his morbid suspicions, would he believe her? If belief is taking a propositional attitude, he would. The concept of belief is explanatory and causal: it is part of the web of concepts by means of which human action is explained. That you cannot dismiss all suspicions that a belief is false is not incompatible with holding it, provided that you neither assent to them, nor allow them to affect your plans or your conduct.

Plans have an equivocal character: a plan can be thought of either as a sheer result of deliberation, without any further commitment, or as a resolve to put such a result into execution.

Thought of in the former way, a completed plan is equivalent to a belief about how something may possibly be brought about. Making a plan, so understood, can be an action; and so can persevering in the belief that it is practicable. Yet there is a sense in which you cannot plan a plan: namely, that you cannot deliberate about what a specific result of deliberation is; for if you can specify it you have nothing to deliberate about.

Thought of in the latter way, a plan is an intention to put a result of deliberation into execution. And just as you cannot plan an already formed plan, so you cannot intend to form an already formed intention: in forming it you leave no room for a further intention to form it. However, both forming an intention and persisting in one can be full human actions. Just as you can plan to make a plan which you have not already made, so you can intend to form an intention you have not already formed. For example, you can intend to form an intention either to accept or to refuse an offer of a job, or a proposal of marriage, in time to dispatch your acceptance or refusal by the last mail of the day. And you can intend to form a given intention that has some special character over and above being an intention: for example a New Year Resolution, or an intention expressed in doing some special action, such as a priest's intention in offering Mass.

You can also intend to persevere with an intention already formed. When you form an intention, you will normally persist in it until what you intend is brought about, or you will abandon it. However, intentions directed to the distant future often lapse as situations change, and beliefs and wishes with them. Foreseeing this, you may try to arm yourself against it in anticipation, imagining future possibilities and making plans to sustain your intention should they arise.

Since not only formings of both cognitive and appetitive propositional attitudes, but also persistings in them, can be intentional and so full human actions, such actions may be caused by other human actions. Any action that arises from a complex plan, for example, will include actions of planning among its causes. However, in any complex of beliefs and intentions by which a human action is explained, some must be elicited acts, and not full actions. If a given mental action must be, under some description, either an intentional forming of a propositional attitude, or an intentional persisting in one, and if the intendings and believings that explain that action are themselves human actions, then those intendings and believings must themselves be explained by further intendings and believings, and so on. Since it is a commonplace that a series of such explanations that does not come to an end is vicious, the beliefs and intentions by which a non-vicious series is terminated cannot be actions: they must be 'elicited'. The beliefs will presumably be part of the background the agent takes for granted in his thinking; but, as we shall see, his elicited intendings are another matter.

Bodily actions pose a problem that mental ones do not. It is not usual to describe a mental action that causes a bodily one (say, a calculation that causes a bodily movement) as the bringing about of some effect of that bodily one. Yet bodily actions are more often than not described as bringings about of effects outside their agents' bodies, and not seldom of remote effects. Arthur Danto was the first to ask what a bodily action is in itself, stripped of all reference to its effects or circumstances; and he spoke of an action so considered as 'basic' (Brand, 152–4, 157), although he developed his views almost beyond recognition (cf. Danto (2), 12–15, 24).) However, as Davidson pointed out, if actions are individual events, changing the true descriptions we give of them cannot change what we describe. Truly describing an action without referring to any of its effects or circumstances cannot yield a description of a plain 'basic' one underlying a causally and circumstantially bedizened non-basic one. The action described remains what it was; all that has happened is that it is now described in a way that is basic or minimal (Davidson (1), 59–61).

Well, even if bodily actions are what they are, no matter how they are truly described, what would a true description of one that referred neither to its effects or circumstances be like – a basic or minimal *description*? How, for example, could Oedipus' action in striking Laius be described, without referring to its effect on Laius (that he was hit, and not missed), or implicitly to its circumstances (for example, that Oedipus was holding a stick – for it was by his stick that Laius was struck)? Would it be as a certain movement of his arm? But that too was an effect of certain contractions and relaxations of his muscles. And they in their turn were effects, this time of the firing of certain neurons in his central nervous system.

This line of thought, as Davidson has divined, shows that the idea that the nature of a human action is revealed by a basic or minimal description of it, purged of all reference to its effects and circumstances, is incompatible with the Socratic tradition. For if actions are doings that are self-referentially explained by their doers' intentions, and if, as is readily shown, the only concept a doer often has of what he is doing is in terms of effects he intends, then describing his action without reference to its effects will omit something essential to its character as an action.

If Oedipus believed that he had control over whether he would strike the insolent stranger with his stick, but, like all his contemporaries, lacked accurate knowledge of what events in his body (namely, neuron firings) cause the movements of the arm by which it would be done, then, as Davidson has pointed out, he could have intended to bring about those events only under some non-committal description such as *'whatever events in his body would result in a striking of the insolent stranger by his stick, as self-referentially caused by his intention.'* No such description would be basic or minimal; for, although it would identify the bodily events that cause the intended effects, it would do so by referring to those effects. Yet if you are seeking a description under which Oedipus could have intended whatever was the ultimate cause in his body of the peripheral movements that resulted in the insolent stranger's being struck, then what you need, in Davidson's words, is 'not a description that d[oes] not mention the effect, but a description which fit[s] the cause' (Davidson (1), 52).

The possibility of intending to bring about neuron firings in your brain under non-committal descriptions of this kind tempted Davidson, despite his criticism of the concept of a basic or minimal description of an action, to preserve a vestige of it: namely, that what human beings intend, when they intend a bodily action, is always to bring about events in their bodies non-committally described as those that will cause some specific effect they wish for. On his own principles, that was a mistake. If a bodily action is a bodily movement that is self-referentially caused by an intention of the agent in whose body it occurs, then that movement must be one of which the agent believes he is in direct control. The movements of which Oedipus believed he was in direct control were presumably of the kinds of which instructors in the martial arts believe their pupils are in direct control: movements of their limbs, changes of their posture, and placings of their feet. True, had he known that any movement of striking he might make would be caused by changes in his central nervous system, and had he wished to bring about such changes, he could have done so: but only by intending to make such a movement of striking. That was directly in his power. He could have brought about changes in his central nervous system, but only indirectly.

This fact, as Chisholm has pointed out, forbids us to identify actions with their cerebral causes. Since Oedipus' actions are self-referentially caused by his intentions, and since his intentions presuppose that the actions they cause are among those he believes to be under his direct control, they cannot be cerebral processes about his control of which he has no firm beliefs at all. Only if he learns that cerebral processes cause his voluntary bodily movements can he intend to bring them about at all; and then only by bringing about the movements under his control that they cause.

A fanciful parallel would be a driver's control over an automobile of the future, designed to respond to the cerebral processes that go with (or are identical with) its driver's choices. You would drive it by making unambiguous choices about what it should do on the road: turn right, turn left, and so on. In choosing that it turn right, you would bring about a series of events in its steering system that would cause it to turn right. You need have no beliefs whatever about what those events are, and even if you had, it would not respond to choices that its working parts function in this way or that, because it is not designed to. You could make its steering mechanism cause it to turn right: but only by choosing that it turn right (cf. Chisholm (1), 35–6).

It follows that actions by different agents having some true descriptions in common (for example, 'being a shifting into top gear') may not be self-referentially caused by the same choices.

A skilled driver may think of the series of movements he makes as he shifts into top gear as a single process which he carries out automatically as it were; a novice may not be able to co-ordinate how his hands and feet move without careful attention, or make any shift without keeping in his mind's eye the diagram of the movements of the stick needed for it. The choices of the novice and the skilled driver that self-referentially explain their actions in driving will differ as do their beliefs about what they can do as drivers (cf. Chisholm (3), 209).

The causal relation between a choice and the action it explains is of the kind to which most causal theorists in the analytical tradition have devoted all their attention, namely that of the causation of event by event, also called 'occurrent' and 'transient'.

While events may be causally related without their relation being an instance of a law of nature, as Anscombe and Searle have shown, it is also possible that all causal relations between events are in fact instances of laws of nature. Choices and the actions they cause may be instances either of purely physical laws (as materialists believe, whether functionalist or anomalous) or of psychophysical ones (as dualists like C.D. Broad believe). Yet most of those who hold either of these positions go on to draw a further conclusion which few adherents of the Socratic tradition can accept: namely, that the ultimate elicited acts of will and intellect by which choices and hence actions are caused are themselves either uncaused or are in turn caused by events that are neither acts of will nor acts of intellect.

If all causal relations are between events, and if every event has a cause, then every elicited act of will or intellect must be caused by events that are not acts of will or intellect at all. Most contemporary materialists profess not to be disturbed by this. They contend that it is enough that actions are self-referentially caused by choices, and that non-spontaneous choices are caused by wishes and beliefs. True, elicited wishes, beliefs and spontaneous choices have further causes; but that they have them and what they are is not the business of the theory of action.

Even some of those who believe both that all causal relations are between events, and that every event has a cause, are disturbed by this conclusion. Some, like Broad, are not materialists; others, like Searle, are. The line of thought that has most disturbed them is suggested by Aristotle's remark that

> choice cannot exist either without thought and intellect or without a moral state; for good action and its opposite cannot exist without a combination of intellect and character (Aristotle (4), VI, 1139a 33–5).

It is that the ultimate beliefs and wishes that cause your actions are effects of your situation (as you believe it to be) and your character, both cognitive and appetitive. Except in your infancy, your character has been itself affected by your past actions, each of which has in turn been the effect of the situation in which it was done, and your character when you did it. Here, as Benson Mates has remarked, 'it is relevant to ask how [you] came to have that character.' In the case of bad actions it is often asked in order to exculpate the agent by directing attention to the fact that the character he was born with and his situation at birth were completely beyond his control; but it can also be asked in the case of good actions, if ungraciously, in order to point out that the agent's original good character or favourable circumstances were equally beyond his control (Mates, 72).

From an Aristotelian point of view, character cannot be treated in this way because, however it is formed and developed, it does not causally explain action. This is particularly clear in the case of appetitive character. As Kenny has argued, 'Aristotle's point is that a person's *prohairesis* will always *reveal* his moral character: trace a man's practical reasoning up to the end which he sets himself, and you will discover whether he is virtuous, vicious, brutish, foolish, incontinent or whatever' (Kenny (3), 98). Or put another way, a human being should not be thought of as an agent until he is mature enough for his individual actions, however caused, to exhibit his virtues and vices. In treating the wishes that underlie his choices as exemplifying his moral character, Aristotle implicitly denies that it causes them.

If all causal relations are between events, which Aristotle did not maintain, then, given that you have the beliefs you do, the cause of your forming or sticking to a certain wish will be some prior event. Identifying that event with your continuing to have a certain moral character leaves you in the dark about it; for it says no more than that you wish as you do because you are disposed to do so. While not vacuous, any more than it is vacuous to explain your sleeping after taking opium by opium's being a soporific, all it tells you is that, given your beliefs, something we know not what about the state you are in causes you to wish as you do.

Once character is excluded as a cause, a possibility emerges which, despite its roots in everyday forms of speech, horrifies most contemporary students of causation. Chisholm has definitively expounded it, although in terms of a non-Fregean ontology of fact-like entities which he calls states of affairs. Its point of departure is that actions are commonly spoken of as caused, not by other events, but by their agents. Indeed, being done by somebody seems to have been the original concept of causation. As Austin remarked,

> 'Causing', I suppose, was a notion taken from every man's own experience of doing simple actions, and by primitive man every event was construed in terms of this model: every event has a cause, that is every event is an action done by somebody – if not by a man, then by a quasi-man, a spirit (Austin, 202).

Thomas Reid was perhaps the last major philosopher to treat
this as the strict sense of the word 'cause', and the familiar
sense today, that of an occurrent cause, as vulgar and inaccu-
rate (Reid, I, 6/41–5). But even if nobody now would describe
as 'strict' or 'philosophical' the sense of 'cause' in which an
agent who brings about an event is said to cause it, the word
continues to be used in that sense. The philosophical question
is not whether there is such a thing as causation in this sense,
but whether it can be reduced to occurrent causation (cf.
Chisholm (3), 199).

The reason for doubting whether that relation can be so
reduced derives from the conception of appetitive intellectual
power, or will, itself. The powers of non-rational beings, like
the power of moving things to move others, or of hot things to
heat others, are exerted by their very natures. When you place
a kettle of water on a hot stove, the stove has the power to
bring it to the boil, but not the power not to do so. By contrast,
the power of a rational being to choose to swim a mile is
exerted, not by nature, but 'at will'. Suppose that somebody
should laugh at your claim that you can choose to swim a mile,
and should point out that you have never yet chosen to. You
might reply that nevertheless you can: that you swim half a
mile every day, and that you do not choose to swim further
because it becomes too boring. If what you said were true, it
would at least be an open question whether you can choose to
swim double your normal distance or not. It is not settled by
the fact that you do not choose to, as the question whether the
hot stove can bring to the boil the kettle of water placed on it
would be settled if it did not.

Even so, probably a majority of philosophers in the analytic
tradition would say that you cannot. They would acknowledge
both that, under some description, a full human action is
chosen, and that you can do what, if you choose, you would do.
But they would point out that it does not follow that you can
choose differently if your circumstances on the various occa-

sions on which you choose not to swim more than half a mile are exactly repeated, and if you yourself are absolutely unaltered. And they maintain that there is no good reason to believe that you can.

They do not deny that there is a bad reason for believing it, which has been anticipated in what has been said about the presuppositions of choosing to act: namely, that deliberating what to do presupposes that there may be some way within your control of bringing about what you wish; and that control with respect to a contemplated course of action is power to do it *or not*. However, they reject this as a bad reason, because they deny either that deliberating and choosing presuppose control in this sense, or that, even if they did presuppose it, it would follow that you have it.

You wish to move to a more commodious house. You deliberate about what would suit you, and what you can afford; and, having reached rough conclusions about both, look whether anything satisfying those conclusions is to be had. You are shown one that is within your estimates, but offers less than you would like and costs more. You deliberate further about whether to buy it, or wait in the hope that something better will come on the market. You conclude with some hesitation that you should buy, but, after another inspection, choose not to. In going through this process, can you possibly think of your choice, whatever it may turn out to be, as something for which there are sufficient conditions in your beliefs about your situation and your appetitive constitution, so that choosing other than you do would be impossible in the course of nature? I do not see how you can. The purpose of the whole exercise is to arrive at a set of considerations pro and con in the light of which you are prepared to choose what to do.

Choice is not being moved by your felt appetites to do one of the actions you believe, as a result of deliberation, to be in your power. If it were, we could not, as we do, sometimes deliberate well and choose foolishly; and sometimes deliberate foolishly and choose well. Competent deliberation enables us to choose intelligently. And choice implies options. If only one option is in the course of nature open to you, given your circumstances and the kind of person you are, you cannot think of your deliberation about pros and cons as giving you an opportunity to choose. Of course, even in that case, your deliberation would have some effect on what you decided. But if you think of your ruminations about the desirability of the house as preliminaries to an outcome that is necessary in the natural order, you are not thinking of them as practical. When, deliberating how to gratify a wish, you arrive at a practical conclusion, you only appear to choose to act on it if it is not in your power not to choose to, abandoning that wish. You will always have some sort of reason for doing so: but it may be as slight as that after all you cannot be bothered, or as bad as that although you believe that you will hate living in the house, your friends all assure you that it is just the thing for you. Neither deliberation nor desire (felt appetite) determines choice.

Given that deliberating and choosing presuppose that you have the power either to choose in accordance with any conclusion you may reach or not, your situation and the person you are being the same, is that a good reason for accepting that presupposition as true? It seems to me to be a good, but not necessarily a decisive reason. Good, because to the extent we do not accept it, we are in a state of serious cognitive dissonance. Not decisive, because there may be serious objections to it that lead to a different conception of human action. However, I know of no such objection.

Two objections, which are popular, seem to me radically mistaken. One is sociological, the other epistemological.

The sociological one is that if the power of taking intellectual appetitive attitudes is exercised absolutely at will, then human choices, and hence human actions, would be utterly random and unpredictable. If the theory I have developed implies this, then the fact that human action is not unpredictable would be an empirical disproof of it. But it does not. Human choices, according to the theory I have developed, are between options the chooser arrives at by deliberation, and deliberation depends on his elicited beliefs and the various intellectual operations he conducts with respect to them. Elicited beliefs are largely a matter of one's upbringing and personal experience; and intellectual operations are constrained by human beings' normal capacity to recognize the logically obvious. Most human beings of similar experience and upbringing largely agree in opinion, and hence largely agree about what their options are in various kinds of situation. And human beings are often in a position to inform themselves of the varieties of options those whose experience and upbringing differ from theirs will believe themselves to have.

The predictability of human action, to the extent that it is predictable, results from this. We can often know that in situations of certain kinds, certain kinds of people will believe either that they have no serious option but to do such and such, or that their only serious options are this or that. When we know as much as that, then even if choices among those options were made by a random procedure such as drawing straws, we could predict what they would be with as good a prospect of success as shrewd practical men would have, and with a rather better one than most social scientists. And sometimes much more than that can be known: for example, what is the order in which the different options are desired, and whether the chooser has exhibited dispositions to choose between options of certain sorts on certain grounds. None of these facts about the options between which choices are made is incompatible with the chooser's absolute power to choose as he will.

The epistemological objection has been succinctly put by Irving Thalberg:

we are unsure what agent-causing is. . . . Therefore . . . I asked
if we have any other model for agent-causing besides human
actions or the 'activity' of inanimate objects. Apparently not.
And our alternative to circularity is the rather unenlightening
position that the immanent relationship may not be further
analysed (Thalberg (2), 229).

Jennifer Hornsby has gone further, developing a suggestion of
von Wright.

[E]ven if it is established that 'action' cannot be fully analysed
in terms of psychological notions and event causality . . . [she
writes], that will do nothing to show the propriety of agent
causation as a constituent in an analysis, because we do not
have any understanding of *agent causation* except as we understand *action* (Hornsby, 101; cf. von Wright, 191–2).

This point would be persuasive if Reid and Chisholm invoked
the concept of agent causation to elucidate their theory rather
than as a summary of it. But as far as I understand them, they
do not.

They analyse agency in terms of two concepts, the second of
which I have refined: (1) that of having power to choose
between options presented by deliberation; and (2) that of
being such that, when what one presupposes in choosing is
true, one's choosing self-referentially causes the happening of
what was chosen, whether it be bodily or mental. The concepts
presuppose a distinction between two kinds of power: power
exerted by virtue of the nature and the circumstances of
whatever has it; and power exercised at will. An agent's power
to choose is exercised at will; and if what he presupposes in
choosing is true, his choice causes the chosen action by virtue
of his nature and circumstances. The concept of power, and
the distinction between its kinds, are old explanatory concepts.
And using them in this way to analyse action, since it may be
false, is not empty. If it is true, therefore, it is enlightening.

I have not attempted to explain further the concept of a

power to choose that can be exercised at will. As for whether ascribing that power to human agents is true, I contend only that if we do not, we cannot elucidate the place of appetitive intellectual attitudes in everyday explanations of human action. Of course, I do not know how that power 'works'. Why should I – or Reid or Chisholm? No account can yet be given of how any of the four accepted fundamental physical forces works; but that does not entitle philosophers hostile to the truth-claims of physics to dispense with concepts of those forces in giving an account of what they call the *Lebenswelt*. The concept of a power that is exercised at will underlies the Socratic explanations of action that are not only endorsed in most cultures, but are practically indispensable in our understanding of one another. That no account can yet be given of how such a power works does not entitle philosophers to dispense with the concept of it, if they continue to employ that concept in practice, and have no serious substitute for it in theory.

It is regrettable that the concept of 'agent' or 'non-occurrent' causation is sometimes (not by Chisholm) spoken of as though it elucidates that of a power that is exercised at will. It does not. It only distinguishes explanations in terms of that power from those in terms of causal relations between events. And it is true that human beings are the only putative examples we yet have of possessors of powers that are exercised at will. But human action is of great importance and interest to human beings, and if it can be understood only by employing a concept that applies to nothing else in their experience, they have no option but to employ it.

CHAPTER 10

FREEDOM OF CHOICE

The modern philosophical debate about the freedom of the will, which seems to have begun by an exchange between Hobbes and Bishop Bramhall, has long since degenerated into a dialogue of the deaf; and nothing is to be gained by joining it. Those who applaud Hobbes's *Questions concerning Liberty, Necessity and Chance* applaud Daniel Dennett's *Elbow Room*. And they shake their heads over the benighted souls who cannot grasp the truth plainly declared to them by the great cloud of witnesses that includes Hume, J.S. Mill. G.E. Moore (in one phase), Dickinson Miller (writing as R.E. Hobart), and Paul Marhenke (writing as the University of California Associates). Those who applaud Thomas Reid's defence of Bramhall's position in *Essays on the Active Powers of the Human Mind* applaud Peter van Inwagen's *Essay on Free Will*. (This, and Benson Mates's chapter in his *Skeptical Essays*, are the best recent studies of the topic.) And they in turn are bewildered by the inability of Hobbes's admirers to perceive what is evident to another cloud of witnesses: one that includes William James, R.M. Chisholm, Austin Farrer and G.E.M. Anscombe.

The theory of human action developed in the preceding chapters places me on one of the sides in this barren dialogue: that of Bramhall and Reid. It implies that, if something a human being does is a full human action, it must be unconditionally in his power not only not to do it, but also not to choose to do it. And if that is so, then Reid was right when he maintained that human beings when they act are free, as he defined being free: that is, they have the unconditional power to will what they do, or not to will it (Reid, IV, 1, 259). Since I have nothing to add to the reasons for this that I have given already, I have nothing further directly to contribute to the controversy. However, C.D. Broad has shown that, by a semantic ascent, a better view of its nature can be obtained (cf. Broad, 195–217); and something remains to be learned indirectly by following his example.

Those who have the very small amount of intellectual sympathy needed for understanding the position of Bramhall and Reid are apt to be astonished by the two most popular lines on which, from Hobbes to Dennett, it has been attacked. The first is that the very concept of an unconditional power either to will to do something or not to will it is unintelligible. The second is that, intelligible or not, nobody would imagine that human beings have such a power unless he were duped by some philosophical equivalent of tales about bugbears – 'imaginary being[s] invoked by nurses to frighten children' (Dennett, 4, *n*.1).

The first line has two branches. One is that there is no concept at all of an unconditional power either to will to do something or not to will it. A difference in what you will must be conditional upon some difference in your situation or internal state. Anybody who imagines that he has a concept of an unconditional power to will or not to will is simply deluded, as he would be if he imagined that he had the concept of an intelligent fried egg. Hume and the logical positivists were enamoured of this branch. Its drawback is that the reasons given for pronouncing that no concept corresponds to an expression that some people find dispensable are apt to entail that none corresponds to expressions that everybody finds indispensable, like 'substance' and 'cause'. This emboldened Reid to dismiss objections to his concept of active power as discredited by their absurd implications in parallel cases (cf. Reid, I, 2, 20). Such boldness is rewarded. Although he rejects Chisholm's contemporary restatement of Reid as an obscure and panicky metaphysical response to a cognitive illusion, not even Dennett ventures to deny that Reid and Chisholm have a concept, however mysterious he may think it (Dennett, 76).

The second branch of the objection that there is no intelligible concept of an unconditional power either to will something or not to will it is not that there is no such concept at all, but that it is inconsistent, like the concept of the largest prime number. Broad, for example, maintaining that the concept of such a power presupposes that there is causation that is non-occurrent, went on to argue that the concept of a non-occurrent cause is inconsistent, because such a cause would produce its effect at a particular time, and yet, as non-occurrent, it would remain unexplained why it should produce it then rather than before or after (Broad, 215–16).

Like all arguments for the inconsistency of the concept of a non-occurrent cause known to me, Broad's presupposes that the concept of non-occurrent causation would be defective if it is such that non-occurrent causes do not have all the explanatory power of occurrent causes. But he was not entitled to presuppose that. A continuing being possessed of an unconditional power either to choose or not to choose can be thought of as the cause of its choices; but conceiving it as the cause of a given choice *ex hypothesi* can explain neither why it chose at all, as opposed to not choosing, nor *a fortiori*, why it chose when it did, and not at some other time. It does not, however, follow that the concept of a non-occurrent cause is defective in any way, much less that it is inconsistent.

The first line of attack is now out of favour in both its branches. But the second is all the rage: namely, that unless he were deluded by some bit of philosophical nonsense – by a philosophical bugbear – nobody would imagine that human beings, without some difference of circumstances or inner constitution, have the power either to will something or not to will it. The tactical principles for attacking on this line are two. First, ignore the arguments which the victims of the delusion give – otherwise you will be entangled in the sort of futile and interminable exchange that results from trying to reason a paranoiac out of his suspicions. And secondly, seek the delusion's irrational source, and expose it. With any unwary victim, the following approach is often effective. Begin by searching his writings for some informal illustration that does not exactly fit the case of choice: he may, for example, somewhere have likened being unable to choose otherwise to being compelled to choose. Then, having found one, no matter how vehemently he objects, insist not only that he believes that his illustration is exact, but that his belief that it is exact is the real source of his opinion. Since he is deluded, how would he know the real source of his beliefs?

With wary opponents, the best advice is to ignore everything they say except their deluded avowals. Those seeking a model of how to proceed against the wariest of the wary can find one in Dennett's assault on Chisholm's conclusion that 'we have a prerogative which some would attribute only to God: each of us, when we act, is a prime mover unmoved' (Chisholm (2), 23). No doubt whether this is an illusion is countenanced. 'What factors contributed to producing it?' is the only question that is allowed to arise. Predictably, several such factors are discovered. However, in the twenty-odd pages devoted to searching for them, Chisholm's name is mentioned only once (in alluding to his 'frankly mysterious doctrine of something like *absolute agenthood*'), and his reasons not at all (Dennett, 76–100).

Since anybody following such tactics may look more like a Soviet psychiatrist writing about political deviation than a philosopher disposing of opinions he considers false, Dennett does what he can to dispel that appearance.

> I do not [he protests] mean to suggest that philosophers have deliberately and knowingly fanned the coals of anxiety, or that they have disingenuously exploited that anxiety to provide the spurious motivation for their metaphysical exercises. We philosophers are more the victims than the perpetrators of the induced delusions (Dennett, 4).

We philosophers – but not we in the tradition of Hobbes!

While these tactics are not ineffective in keeping up the spirits of one's own side, that is all that can be said for them. To the extent that sentiment lingers for pursuing philosophy by give and take, Dennett's diagnoses of Chisholm's ailments can neither be addressed to him, nor expect a reply. Diagnoses are directed to fellow-physicians, not to patients; and these are not therapeutic. Ridicule may silence. It does not cure.

You can learn from the writings of Reid and Chisholm what reasons Hobbes and Hume gave for their views about action and will. Yet except for Thalberg and Hornsby, I can think of no adversary of Reid's or Chisholm's theory of agency from whose writings you can learn the reasons they give for it. It is true that those reasons are simple, so simple that it is misleading to describe them as arguments. For example, put in everyday English instead of in his exact technical vocabulary, Chisholm believes that when a human being acts there is no sufficient causal condition of his willing either to do what he does or of his not willing it, because he takes that to be an obvious corollary of his belief that a human being is free either to will to do what he does or not to will it. As we shall see, some deny this; but on the face of it it is gobbledygook to say both that it is in my power to choose or not to choose, and also that sufficient conditions obtain for the occurrence of one of these options and for the non-occurrence of the other (cf. Anscombe (2), II, 145–6; Mates, 64–5, 97).

Further, Chisholm believes that a human being is free to will as he does or not, because he takes that to be an obvious corollary of his analysis of human actions as exercises of their agents' power to do much that they do, or not to do it, as they freely will (cf. Chisholm (1), 84–6; 201– 3). He does not defend the validity of these two inferences, because he takes it to be evident. Rather, he defends the general character of his analysis of human action as a 'one of those things we have a right to believe about ourselves – at least until we have a positive reason for believing them to be false'; and he invites those who do not believe it to supply such a reason (Chisholm (2), 200).

In conducting himself in this simple and straightforward way, Chisholm follows the example of Reid, who also began with an analysis of the concept of active power, which he took to be commonly accepted.

> [Active] power to produce any effect [he wrote] implies power not to produce it. We can conceive no way in which power may be determined to one of these rather than another, in a being that has no will (Reid, I, 5, 35).

Later, in amplifying this remark so that it anticipated Chisholm's position, Reid did give a reason: namely, that

> to say that what depends upon the will is in a man's power, but the will is not in his power, is to say that the end is in his power, but the means necessary to that end are not in his power, which implies a contradiction (Reid, IV, 1, 266).

This reason, however, merely elucidates what he means from the beginning by 'active power'. And he took for granted that nobody would seriously deny that human beings do have active power to do or not to do some things.

These definitions and elucidations are not arbitrary. They are reminders of what, as Austin once put it, is commonly said and presumably thought about human action. And they are important, less because many of us believe them, than because they express what even more of us presuppose in choosing what to do. When Descartes wrote that 'the will simply consists in our ability to do or not do something (that is, to affirm or deny, to pursue or avoid)' (Descartes, VII, 57), and when Dr Johnson declared to Boswell, 'Sir, the will is free, and there's an end on't,' they likewise were expressing something they took their contemporaries to presuppose in choosing what to do. Making that presupposition was part of the culture they inherited, and which is still being transmitted. Inventing arguments for it misrepresents its place in the thinking of those who share that culture.

Further evidence that Reid and Chisholm have correctly stated something that is presupposed in much common practical thinking may be found in the testimony of an impressive array of thinkers who acknowledge the soundness of causal arguments against it. Broad, Mates and Searle are three such witnesses. One of the greatest of the Victorians, the applied mathematician William Kingdon Clifford, was another. His *Lectures and Essays* contains a statement of 'the doctrine of free will, as commonly understood' upon which I have already drawn, namely:

> Whenever a man exercises his will, and makes a voluntary choice of one out of various possible courses, an event occurs, whose relation to contiguous events cannot be included in a general statement applicable to all similar cases. There is something wholly capricious and arbitrary, belonging to that moment only; and we have no right to conclude that if circumstances were exactly repeated, and the man himself absolutely unaltered, he would choose the same course (Clifford, 318).

Those who accept the doctrine Clifford formulates will no doubt contest his description of exercises of the will as capricious and arbitrary; but not the formulation by which he would defend it.

Unfortunately, the freedom of choice as commonly understood is sometimes defended, not as a presupposition in terms of which human action is conceived in our inherited culture, but as something that can be known by experience. Even Reid in one passage says that it is probable that 'the very conception of active power . . . is derived from our voluntary exertions in producing effects' (Reid, IV, 2/270). And Searle has asserted it in the strongest terms.

> [I]f there is any fact of experience that we are all familiar with, it's the simple fact that our own choices, decisions, reasonings, and cognitions seem to make a difference to our actual behaviour. There are all sorts of experiences that we have in life where it seems just a fact of our experience that though we did one thing, we feel we know perfectly well that we could have done something else. We know we could have done something else, because we chose one thing for certain reasons. But we were aware that there were also reasons for choosing something else, and indeed, we might have acted on those reasons and chosen that something else (Searle (2), 87–8).

This admirably catches what many of us presuppose when we deliberate about what to do, but I have already argued that it is not from our experience that we learn to presuppose it. On the contrary, we presuppose it in reporting what we experience.

When I exercise my ability to choose, I do not experience my power to exercise that ability otherwise, as I may experience my choice as pleasant or difficult. Young children and animals experience pain and difficulty, while having neither words for them nor concepts of them. But if experiencing being able to choose otherwise than I do is anything more than being aware of making a choice and believing that I could have refrained from making it, I have no idea what it could be. Of course, since I believe that I cannot make a choice unless it is in my power not to make it, my avowals of the choices I make are in terms of that belief. But if I did not believe it, I do not see what in my immediate experience could justify my believing it. Human beings' percepts of their actions would be blind without concepts of cognitive and appetitive propositional attitudes; and any such concepts will presuppose various things about their power to take those attitudes, and about how taking them affects behaviour.

If human beings credit themselves with power to choose or not to choose what they do, and many of them do credit themselves with it, it is because the body of concepts and beliefs in terms of which they think about their actions implies that they have it. The traditional Aristotelian theory of action, as developed in the Middle Ages, was an attempt to elucidate, refine and enlarge that body. And that theory has, in turn, contributed much to the way in which action is described in modern everyday speech, not least by introducing the word 'intend' and its cognates. Hence it should not surprise us that various practical commonplaces are elementary corollaries of different parts of the traditional theory. Nor should it surprise us that those who reject that theory and its implication about the freedom of choice should wish to reinterpret, in terms of some more palatable theory, as much as possible of the way human action is commonly spoken and thought about.

A doctrine has therefore emerged that is now familiar enough to have an agreed name, 'compatibilism'. According to it, ascribing to human beings the power to choose or not to choose as they do is compatible with there being sufficient causal conditions of their choosing as they do, that is, with their not choosing as they do being impossible in the course of nature. Instead of taking the strong Hobbist line that human beings are free to do what they do or not as they choose, but not to choose or not to choose to do it, compatibilism affirms that they can choose or not choose to do it, but not in the sense of the traditional theory, according to which, if they can either choose or not, then both their choosing and their not choosing must be possible in the course of nature.

That the expression 'being able to choose or not' can be

given a compatibilist sense should be uncontroversial. When
Alice, in *Through the Looking-Glass*, expressed a doubt whether
you can make words mean different things, Humpty-Dumpty
properly told her that the question is which is to be master –
that's all. Several compatibilist senses of 'being able to choose
or not' have been proposed; for there are several compatibilist
theories of action. But exercising our mastery over what our
words mean does not help us to answer such philosophical
questions as whether your choice to have a second cup of coffee
was a propositional attitude it was in your power not to take,
even though your circumstances and internal state were
exactly as they were when you took it. If it was, it would not
matter in the least that there is a compatibilist sense of 'being
able to choose or not' in which, even though you could only not
have chosen it had your internal state been different, you could
nevertheless be said to have been able either to choose to take a
second cup or not. And if it was not, it would not matter in the
least that the customary sense of 'being able to choose or not' is
not compatibilist. Disputes about compatibilism distract
attention from this limitation of our power as masters of the
words we use.

An acceptable philosophical theory of action must be consistent with what it is reasonable to believe about human beings'
power to choose to act. I have argued that the version of the
traditional Aristotelian theory I have developed is consistent
with what has been traditionally presupposed about it in the
culture we have inherited, and that according to that theory,
human beings' power to choose to do what they believe to be in
their power, or not to choose to do it, is unconditional. Is it
reasonable to believe what has traditionally been presupposed? Yes, unless reasons can be given for disbelieving it. As
far as I know, only two such reasons are now seriously offered.

The first is metaphysical. It is that, for every event, there
must be sufficient conditions why it occurred rather than did
not occur. Hence, for any human choice, if sufficient condi-

tions for its being made occur, then it must be impossible in the course of nature that it not be made; and if sufficient conditions for its not being made occur, it is similarly impossible that it be made. This position is a form of what is known as 'determinism'. It has been economically stated by Benson Mates, as follows.

> [O]ur basic metaphysical picture of the world requires us to admit that, whenever anybody does anything, it is the case that anybody else *in those very same circumstances* would have done the same thing . . . It looks as though the only real difference between the actions we excuse and those we see fit to punish is that in the former case we know enough about the causal background to appreciate the inevitability, whereas in the latter case our ignorance of the background allows us to say, casually and irresponsibly, 'He could and should have done otherwise' (Mates, 66).

It is, however, a mistake to describe this metaphysical picture as 'ours', if the implicit 'we' refers to all competent philosophers (Chisholm and Anscombe, for example); and a worse mistake if it refers to human beings at large.

Yet Mates rightly dismisses the anti-determinist objection that 'human actions are somehow exempt from the same kinds of causal connections that characterize the rest of nature' as 'patently untenable and completely ad hoc' (Mates, 62). However, asserting human freedom of choice does not imply that. Its two pertinent corollaries are, first, that the choices that largely determine how human beings behave do not, according to the laws of any natural science, known or unknown, have prior physical or mental events as their sufficient conditions; and hence, secondly, that the known laws of nature are not such as to exclude that possibility. The second of these corollaries, at least, is undeniable.

It is not clear whether Mates has a metaphysical proof of his determinist picture in mind; or, if he has, which one. The

considerations advanced in support of it by Hobbes and Hume
are not formidable; and the different premises by which
Spinoza and Kant essayed to demonstrate it now command
little assent. Yet its recent history shows how tenacious of it
many philosophers are.

At the turn of the present century, it was presupposed in
physics that, if two physical situations are identical in every
physical respect, then they must have identical outcomes; and
although on the face of it, two identical animals (not necessarily human ones) can be in exactly the same internal condition
and external circumstances and yet behave differently, this
appearance was put down to our ignorance. Sidgwick vividly
depicted the advance of science as having already so contracted the region of situations the outcomes of which are
causally undetermined that little more than the 'citadel' of the
will remains unreduced. He could not know that, a bare half
century after his death, quantum electrodynamics would
assert that the contrary is true: that identical physical situations can have different outcomes. But had he known it, he
would have been astonished that philosophers who accepted
the deterministic picture of the world would respond to it by
jettisoning their former argument for that picture, and would
maintain (correctly, as a matter of logic) that determinism
may be true of macro-events even if it is not of micro ones. For,
metaphysics apart, the only reason there had ever been for
believing that it was true of all macro-events was that physics
is deterministic. It was not metaphysics that determinists
invoked in the days of their glory.

When physics was deterministic, determinism was irresistible by reductive materialists, even though there are enormous
tracts of animal and human behaviour for which neither
biology nor psychology furnishes deterministic explanations.
But now that physics is not deterministic, it is hard to find
even reductive materialist reasons for asserting that every
human choice must have sufficient conditions, in face of the

fact that no science has ever pretended, even in theory, to establish what they are.

The second line on which it is possible to argue that the human beings do not have an unconditional power to choose to do what is in their power to do, or not to choose it, is not deterministic. It has been most effectively followed by Searle. He expressly repudiates the assumption that identical physical situations must have identical outcomes (Searle (1), 117–20). Nor does he resort to metaphysics. Instead, he looks, as the Victorians rightly did, to 'the contemporary scientific view'. According to that view, he declares,

> all of the surface features of the world are entirely caused by and realised in systems of micro-elements, the behaviour of [which] is sufficient to determine everything that happens. Such a 'bottom up' picture of the world allows for 'top-down' causation (our minds, for example, can affect our bodies). But top-down causation only works because the top level is already caused by and realised in the bottom levels (Searle (2), 94).

This position does not imply that, if a micro-situation that is the same in all respects as an earlier one occurs, then it must be followed by one of exactly the same kind as that which followed it before. It implies only that, whatever kind of micro-situation follows it, it 'bottom up' causes a macro-situation of exactly the same kind as micro-situations of that kind always do; and that whatever explanation there may be of that micro-situation is wholly in the province of micro-physics.

That in turn implies that what human beings choose depends on what micro-events occur in their central nervous systems, they being non-deterministically explained by earlier micro-events. Whether micro-events of a certain kind occur or not cannot depend on whether or not a human being chooses something. It appears to do so only to those who forget that choices that 'top-down' cause bodily events are themselves realized in micro-events, and that those micro-events are in the end non-deterministically explained by earlier micro-events that are not 'top-down' caused by any choice at all.

Is Searle right about what the contemporary scientific view is? He may be, if 'the contemporary scientific view' about any matter is the opinion about it a random sampling of readers of *The Scientific American* have somehow picked up, without making use of it in any scientific work they do. But, so understood, contemporary scientific views about most matters on which research is being done have little authority: indeed, one of the functions of *The Scientific American* is to correct those views by reporting on that research. If, on the other hand, the contemporary scientific view about something is what is accepted about it in up-to-date research on it, then there is reason to suppose that Searle is mistaken.

Science as an enterprise is diverse, critical and free-thinking. In every field, 'bottom up' explanations are given and prized. But in large parts of biology, ecology and the social sciences they are neither available nor seriously sought, and in some they are at present inconceivable. It is therefore untrue that all work in biology, ecology or the social sciences presupposes that there are 'bottom up' explanations in micro-events for everything that happens. On the contrary, no research programme in the sciences in any way forbids those who engage in it to believe that they were unconditionally free not to have chosen to, and that their choice cannot be explained as the outcome either of sufficient micro-conditions, or of a throw of micro-dice (cf. van Inwagen, 197–202).

It cannot be denied that advances in science may invalidate action theory in the Socratic tradition as they have already invalidated ancient Greek theories of motion and causation. The notion that philosophy should be kept pure of any tincture of science, or that it can be, has never been effectively defended. Yet philosophers should beware of mistaking current vulgarities about science, or science fiction, for the real thing.

Socrates reminded his friends that there was much they could and did understand about their own and others' actions without the help of physical theory. And he went on to argue that nothing that would be discovered in the physical sciences about the human body and its physical environment would invalidate that understanding. Although much more has been discovered about both than he could have imagined, his prediction so far stands. Discoveries to come may, it is true, invalidate it; but as yet there is no reason to anticipate that they will.

BIBLIOGRAPHY

Anscombe, G.E.M. (1), *Intention*, 2nd edn, Oxford: Blackwell, 1966.

Anscombe, G.E.M. (2), *Collected Papers*, 3 vols, Oxford: Blackwell, 1981.

Aquinas, St Thomas (1), *Summa Theologiae*, 60 vols, London: Eyre & Spottiswoode, 1964–76.

Aquinas, St Thomas (2), *Aristotle's de Anima . . . [with] the Commentary of St Thomas Aquinas*, tr. Kenelm Foster and Silvester Humphries, London: Routledge & Kegan Paul, 1951.

Aristotle (1), *de Anima*, tr. in Barnes, Jonathan (ed.).

Aristotle (2), *de Motu Animalium*, tr. in Barnes, Jonathan (ed.).

Aristotle (3), *Metaphysics*, tr. in Barnes, Jonathan (ed.).

Aristotle (4), *Nicomachean Ethics*, tr. in Barnes, Jonathan (ed.).

Audi, Robert, 'Intending', *Journal of Philosophy*, 70 (1973): 387–403.

Aune, Bruce, *Reason and Action*, Dordrecht: Reidel, 1977.

Austin, J.L., *Philosophical Papers*, 2nd edn, Oxford: Clarendon Press, 1970.

Barnes, Jonathan (ed.), *The Complete Works of Aristotle: the Revised Oxford Translation*, 2 vols, Princeton, N.J.: Princeton University Press, 1984.

Barwise, Jon and Perry, John, *Situations and Attitudes*, Cambridge, Mass.: MIT Press, 1983.

Brand, Myles, 'Particulars, Events and Actions', in Brand and Walton.

Brand, Myles and Walton, Douglas (eds), *Action Theory*, Dordrecht: Reidel, 1980.

Bratman, Michael (1), 'Two Faces of Intention', *Philosophical Review*, 93 (1984): 375–405.

Bratman, Michael (2), 'Davidson's Theory of Intention', in Vermazen and Hintikka, 13–26.

Broad, C.D., *Ethics and the History of Philosophy*, London: Routledge & Kegan Paul, 1952.

Castaneda, Hector-Neri (1), *Thinking and Doing: the Philosopical Foundations of Institutions*, Dordrecht: Reidel, 1975.

Castaneda, Hector-Neri (2), 'The Twofold Structure and the Unity of Practical Thinking', in Brand and Walton.

Chisholm, Roderick M. (1), *Person and Object*, London: Allen & Unwin, 1976.

Chisholm, Roderick M. (2), 'Freedom and Action', in Lehrer.

Chisholm, Roderick M. (3), 'The Agent as Cause', in Brand and Walton.

Churchland, Paul M., 'Eliminative Materialism and Propositional Attitudes', *Journal of Philosophy*, 88 (1981): 67– 90.

Clark, Stephen R.L., *The Nature of the Beast*, Oxford: Oxford University Press, 1982.

Clifford, William Kingdon, *Lectures and Essays*, ed. Leslie Stephen and Frederick Pollock, London: Macmillan, 1879.

Collingwood, R.G., *The Idea of Nature*, Oxford: Clarendon Press, 1945.

Cottingham, John, Stoothoff, Robert and Murdoch, Dugald (eds and trs.), *The Philosophical Writings of Descartes*, 2 vols, Cambridge: Cambridge University Press, 1985.

Danto, Arthur C. (1), *Analytical Philosophy of Action*, Cambridge: Cambridge University Press, 1973.

Danto, Arthur C. (2), 'Action, Knowledge and Representation', in Brand and Walton.

Davidson, Donald (1), *Essays on Actions and Events*, Oxford:

Clarendon Press, 1980.

Davidson, Donald (2), *Inquiries into Truth and Interpretation*, Oxford: Clarendon Press, 1984.

Davidson, Donald (3), Contributions to Vermazen and Hintikka.

Descartes, René, *Oeuvres de Descartes*, 11 vols, ed. Charles Adam and Paul Tannery, Paris: Vrin (with CRNS), 1964–74. Texts quoted tr. in Cottingham, Stoothoff and Murdoch (eds and trs.).

Dretske, F.I., 'Can Events Move?' *Mind*, 76 (1967): 479–92.

Dummett, Michael (1), *Frege: Philosophy of Language*, 2nd edn, London: Duckworth, 1981.

Dummett, Michael (2), *The Interpretation of Frege's Philosophy*, London: Duckworth, 1981.

Fodor, Jerry A., *Representations*, Cambridge, Mass.: MIT Press, 1981.

Frankfurt, Harry G., 'The Problem of Action', *American Philosophical Quarterly*, 15 (1978): 157–62.

Frege, Gottlob (1), 'Ueber Sinn und Bedeutung', *Zeitschrift fuer Philosophie und philosophische Kritik*, 100 (1892): 25– 50. Tr. in McGuinness (ed.). [Page refs to original (on left) and to McGuinness.]

Frege, Gottlob (2), 'Der Gedanke', *Beitraege zur Philosophie des deutschen Idealismus*, 1 (1918): 58–77. Tr. in McGuinness (ed.). [Page refs. to original (on left) and to McGuinness.]

Frege, Gottlob (3), *Philosophical and Mathematical Correspondence*, ed. G. Gabriel and others; abridged B. McGuinness and tr. H. Kaal. Oxford: Blackwell, 1980.

Geach, P.T. (1), *Mental Acts*, London: Routledge & Kegan Paul, 1957.

Geach, P.T. (2), *Logic Matters*, Oxford: Blackwell, 1972.

Goldman, Alvin I., *A Theory of Human Action*, Englewood Cliffs, N.J.: Prentice-Hall, 1970.

Hintikka, Merrill, see Vermazen and Hintikka.

Hochberg, Herbert, *Thought, Fact, and Reference*, Minneapolis:

University of Minnesota Press, 1978.

Horgan, Terence and Woodward, James, 'Folk Psychology is Here to Stay', *Philosophical Review*, 94 (1985): 197–226.

Hornsby, Jennifer, *Actions*, London: Routledge & Kegan Paul, 1980.

Kenny, Anthony (1), *Action, Emotion and Will*, London: Routledge & Kegan Paul, 1963.

Kenny, Anthony (2), *Will, Freedom and Power*, Oxford: Blackwell, 1975.

Kenny, Anthony (3), *Aristotle's Theory of the Will*, London: Duckworth, 1979.

Lehrer, Keith (ed.), *Freedom and Determinism*, New York: Random House, 1966.

Linsky, Leonard, *Oblique Contexts*, Chicago: Chicago University Press, 1983.

Mates, Benson, *Skeptical Essays*, Chicago: University of Chicago Press, 1981.

McGuinness, Brian (ed.), *Gottlob Frege: Collected Papers on Mathematics, Logic and Philosophy*, Oxford: Blackwell, 1985.

Murdoch, Dugald, see Cottingham, Stoothoff and Murcoch.

O'Shaughnessy, Brian, *The Will: a Dual Aspect Theory*, 2 vols, Cambridge: Cambridge University Press, 1980.

Perry, John, see Barwise and Perry.

Plato, *Phaedo*, in *Euthyphro, Apology, Crito, Phaedo and Phaedrus*, text with translation by Harold North Fowler, Loeb Classical Library, London: Heinemann, 1926.

Quine, Willard van Orman (1), *Word and Object*, Cambridge, Mass.: MIT Press, 1960.

Quine, Willard van Orman (2), *Theories and Things*, Cambridge, Mass.: Harvard University Press, 1981.

Reid, Thomas, *Essays on the Active Powers of the Human Mind*, Cambridge, Mass.: MIT Press, 1969. [Numerical refs. to essay, section, and page.]

Russell, Bertrand (1), *Logic and Knowledge*, ed. Robert C. Marsh, London: Allen & Unwin, 1956.

Russell, Bertrand (2), *An Inquiry into Meaning and Truth*, London: Allen & Unwin, 1940.

Ryle, Gilbert, *The Concept of Mind*, London: Hutchinson, 1949.

Searle, John (1), *Intentionality*, Cambridge: Cambridge University Press, 1983.

Searle, John (2), *Minds, Brains, and Science*, Cambridge, Mass.: Harvard University Press, 1984.

Sellars, Wilfrid (1), 'Thought and Action', in Lehrer.

Sellars, Wilfrid (2), 'Volitions Reaffirmed', in Brand and Walton.

Smart, J.J.C., 'Davidson's Minimal Materialism', in Vermazen and Hintikka.

Stich, Stephen P., *From Folk Psychology to Cognitive Science*, Cambridge, Mass.: MIT Press, 1984.

Stoothoff, Robert, see Cottingham, Stoothoff and Murdoch.

Stoutland, Frederick (1), 'The Logical Connection Argument', in *American Philosophical Quarterly: Monograph Series*, No.4, Oxford: Blackwell, 1970.

Stoutland, Frederick (2), 'Oblique Causation and Reasons for Action', *Synthèse* 43 (1980): 351–67.

Thalberg, Irving (1), *Perception, Emotion and Action*, Oxford: Blackwell, 1977.

Thalberg, Irving (2), 'How Does Agent Causality Work?' in Brand and Walton.

van Inwagen, Peter, *An Essay on Free Will*, Oxford: Clarendon, 1983.

Vermazen, Bruce and Hintikka, Merrill B., *Essays on Davidson: Actions and Events*, Oxford: Clarendon, 1985.

von Wright, Georg Henrik, *Explanation and Understanding*, Ithaca: Cornell University Press, 1971.

Watson, James D. *The Double Helix*, New York: Signet Books, 1969.

White, Alan R., *Attention*, Oxford: Blackwell, 1964.

Wilkes, K.V., *Physicalism*, London: Routledge & Kegan Paul, 1981.

Wittgenstein, Ludwig (1), *Tractatus Logico-Philosophicus*, tr. D.F. Pears and Brian McGuinness, London: Routledge & Kegan Paul, 1961.

Wittgenstein, Ludwig (2), *Philosophical Investigations*, tr. G.E.M. Anscombe, 3rd edn. Oxford: Blackwell, 1967.

Wittgenstein, Ludwig (3), *On Certainty*, ed. G.E.M. Anscombe and G.H. von Wright; tr. Denis Paul and G.E.M. Anscombe, Oxford: Blackwell, 1969.

Woodward, James, see Horgan, Terence and Woodward, James.

INDEX